AF430596

A PRINCE

FROM THE ASHES

WRITTEN BY

DREW MEYER

Copyright © 2021 by **Drew Meyer**

All rights reserved. No part of this publication may be reproduced, distributed or transmitted in any form or by any
means, without prior written permission.

Printed by Kindle Direct Publishing, An Amazon.com Company
Drew Meyer Press
3805 Calhoun Ave.
Ames, IA 50010

Unless otherwise specified, Scripture quotations used in this book are taken from the 2016 edition of the Holy Bible, English Standard Version®. ESV®. Copyright © by Crossways Bibles, Wheaton, IL.

Scripture quotations marked NLT are from the NLT® Bible (Holy Bible, New Living Translation®. Copyright © by
Tyndale House Publishers, Carol Stream, IL.

Book Layout © 2021 BookDesignTemplates.com
Cover Design: Drew Meyer

A Prince from the Ashes / Drew Meyer. -- 1st ed.
ISBN 979-8558898262

I dedicate this book to my Dad, Dean Meyer. Thank you, Dad, for giving me a front row seat to your walk with God. I'm thankful I was raised in an environment where I experienced the love of God at a young age.

Contents

Foreword

by Joy Schroeder

What event or circumstance could shake you? My husband, Dick, and I have been missionaries with Chi Alpha Campus Ministries for over forty years. After our first fifteen years or so, Dick was invited to consider a different position in a different city. He would never insist on the move, but I tried to be open to the possibility. The city sidewalks and the ministry building contained significant barriers for my disability. The ministry targeted different people than the college students we felt called to. I did not want to go there. In fact, I was surprised at how deeply the idea shook me.

My grounding in the Father's love for me as His child had been tested and held firm. But this was a different challenge. I felt like a tree where the soil had collapsed from around my roots, and now I was wobbly. Somehow my roots needed to push down past the gap and find deeper solid ground. That night I prayed, "Father, I'm afraid and insecure. I've reached the depths of what I know about your love for me. Please give me a deeper revelation. I can't do it myself. Will you send my roots deeper into your love?"[1]

I awoke in the morning amazed at the deep peace in my soul. The circumstance had not changed–something had shifted in me. While I was sleeping, He established my identity more deeply in His love. No matter what happened next, I was His child, deeply rooted and held firmly in the love of the Father. Nothing could change that reality. *"And I pray that you, being rooted and established in love, may have power... to grasp how wide and long and high and deep is the love of Christ..."* (Eph. 3:17-19, NIV). Dick decided not to accept the invitation, but the important, grounding work God did that night has held firm through other shaking circumstances. Drew's book contains a quote from this experience.

We met Drew when he was the State Director of Chi Alpha in Iowa. He invited Dick to do a tour of the Iowa Chi Alpha ministries and invest in the leaders. During their rich conversations in the car, Dick mentioned that I was a coach and mentor for ministry leaders, and soon afterwards, Drew reached out to me. During our conversations, Drew impressed me as an authentic follower of Jesus. Jesus was not his "profession." Jesus was the center of his life. He was deeply committed to bringing the gospel to those yet to believe and discipling believers firmly in the truth—all through authentic relationships. Primary in his thinking was his relationship with God. As a gifted leader, he had multiple demands competing for his time: Chi Alpha Director of a thriving campus ministry at Iowa State University, traveling throughout the state as Chi Alpha State Director and to raise support as a missionary, husband of his "best friend" (Drew's words), father of lively young children, and various other responsibilities. Yet he made time for—fought for—meaningful time with God. Evidently Drew really believed that who he was and everything he did must flow from an unobstructed connection with God. I am confident that this belief and practice fuels his ministry now as the busy pastor of a growing church.

In this book, Drew takes us on the path he himself travels daily: to know who God is and, in relationship with Him, to know who we are. But establishing this "gospel identity" is not an end in itself. Rather, it is the place from which we partner with God in what He is doing in our corner of this broken world. To accomplish this, Drew introduces us to the three Persons of the Trinity, who we are in relationship with each, the implications for how we live, and why it matters. If, with God's help, we drive our roots deeply into the bedrock of these truths, they will anchor us through circumstances and events that shake us. What does the bedrock look like?

The Father: Through Jesus's atoning death and resurrection, we become the Father's children, adopted and fully loved. Nothing will change that. No circumstance can touch it. Every day we can pray something like, "Father, what are you doing today, and how can I partner with you in it?" Then, show up and pay attention because He is always at work.

Jesus, the Son: It's good to remember the ashes from which Jesus redeemed us—not with self-disqualifying regret but rather with humble gratitude. Remembering keeps us in touch with our own stumble-potential and also with how lost our friends really are without Him. We learn, or should learn, to readily surrender to Jesus's Kingdom rule whenever it collides with our self-will. Why procrastinate when, as soon as we surrender, we experience the resultant paradoxical freedom? As His ambassadors, we intentionally find opportunities to partner with Him in extending His liberating Kingdom to our neighbors and co-workers. Jesus loves everyone.

The Holy Spirit: Drew writes, "The extravagance of God's love is not only the forgiveness of our sins but also the placing of value on that redeemed life to be the host of God's presence." The Holy Spirit, God himself, dwells in us. We can learn to distinguish when He speaks to us and how He leads us. My husband says we are the Holy Spirit's UPS delivery people. We can ask Him what encouragement He has for the co-worker at lunch or a parent at our child's soccer game.

Our identity and our purpose are anchored in who God is, who He says we are, and what He commissions us to do. This book will bring the reader refreshing insights and inspiration to these truths. Drew writes a timely word in these troubled and uncertain times. As a gentle yet firm guide, he shows us the path he walks, assuring us that, though it is sometimes narrow, it is the best path. He helps us become more deeply anchored in God's extravagant love for us. He inspires us to embrace God's call to partner with His grand endeavor on the planet. If we believe these truths, they will help us stand firm in the faith to the end. Enjoy the journey.

Joy Schroeder
Life Coach
Director of Chi Alpha Summer Job Project,
an intensive student leadership program
Author of *Tools for Mentoring*,
a comprehensive discipleship manual
www.toolsformentoring.com

Introduction

Psalm 113:7-8
*"He raises the poor from the dust and lifts the needy
from the ash heap, to make them sit with princes,
with the princes of his people."*

An unknown athiest once wrote, "Did I firmly believe, as millions say they do, that the
knowledge and practice of religion in this life influences destiny in another, religion would mean
to me everything." These words pierced the heart
of a college student named C.T. Studd in 1883. He
then had to admit, "I at once saw that this was the

truly consistent Christian life. When I looked back upon my own life, I saw how inconsistent it had been." [1]

This atheist's statement is right on. If we believed the words we say we do, wouldn't our lives look radically different? Ever since I read that account, I have been challenged with the convicting realities of the truth of the gospel. I have had a desire to live a life that is consistent with the message I profess to believe.

All too often, in my own life and in much of the church around me, I see a huge disconnect between our faith and our daily lives. We find ourselves settling into the notion of a Christianity that is confined to Sundays. Is our faith real? Are we bored and apathetic? Are we anxious even though we hold the answer? Do we have any confidence in the power of the gospel to transform broken situations? Or is doctrine irrelevant to daily life?

This book is an attempt to lead you into an encounter with the love of God. When a person experiences the love of God for themselves, they begin to realize that the gospel is not just a historical story, but it is also a present reality. Revival starts with revitalizing the truths of the gospel in the hearts of people. We see outward impact on our daily lives when God's truth impacts our hearts.

I'm praying this moment happens for everyone who picks up this book—that each one of us would see that God's love is brilliant. His love is extravagant. His love is a radiant light that allows us to properly see Him for Who He is and ourselves before Him. But often, our vision of His love is obscured by brokenness, distractions, or anxiety. This light pollution is real and impacts us all differently. But there is hope, and it is the goodness of God that reveals His radiant beauty and love.

God's love is multifaceted. It's powerfully complex and, because of that, meant to invade every facet of our life. The ocean of God's love is both deep and wide. It's both peace and power. It's both grace and truth. The love of God is both mercy and justice. His love is expressed in ways that are meant to reach us in our depths and bring us to unfathomable heights.

The gospel is the rescue story of Heaven. God has raised me from the ash heap and propped me up with princes in His Kingdom. That is an apt description of my story. And in fact, it's a beautiful description of the story God wants to write in every person's life, including yours. It's a story of the depths of our despair and the glorious heights of redemption. When people encounter the goodness of God revealed in Father, Son, and Holy Spirit, there becomes less space in their life for uncertainty, anxiety, or boredom. The gospel is what makes sense of this world and calls us to rise up out of the mess and be a part of something beautiful.

I grew up in a Christian home, with parents who loved Jesus, in a great church of people who attempted to live out their love for God in their daily lives. None of it was perfect, but I do feel blessed. I gave my heart to Jesus when I was young, eight or nine years old. I experienced tragedy at a young age through the death of my mother, and this caused me to think more about my life before God, which led to my decision to follow Jesus.

But that moment of surrender wasn't a one-time experience of His love. It was the first of a lifetime of moments. I began to realize He wanted to wash over me daily and draw me into a lifelong experience of knowing Him. From year to year, God has shown me a new level of His faithfulness and His patience towards me.

A few years ago, I got the opportunity to receive some one-on-one mentoring from Joy Schroeder. Joy and her husband Dick are spiritual giants and heroes to me and many others. For more than four decades, they have faithfully served college students from the mountains of Montana through discipleship, coaching, speaking at conferences and retreats, and traveling extensively. I was thrilled to have the opportunity to be coached by Joy for a season.

We began to meet via video chat and dive into the dynamics of life and ministry that I was currently facing. At the time, I was ready to unpack some important decisions that were weighing on me. My wife and I were also walking through difficulties in some outside relationships. Joy began to help me unravel the layers of these, one by one, meeting by meeting.

As we peeled back the layers of these issues, I began to realize these troubles were pointing me to a deeper work that Jesus wanted to do in my life. These issues weighed so heavily on me because of gaps in my understanding of His love for me. I had assumed these to be pragmatic issues to be analyzed and addressed. But God revealed to me how all-encompassing His love is, how His message is good news for everything I face in this life.

At one point, she told me, "Any time I sense insecurity, I have reached the depth of my understanding of the love of God." There it was: the gap or disconnect between faith and experience, or what I profess and my daily life. The gap that exists between my experience and the love of God is actually an invitation for me to experience more of Him.

This book invites you into the love of God in a greater way. His love is matchless, and His grace is extravagant.

DIMENSIONS OF GOD'S LOVE

I have chosen to unpack three dimensions of God's love revealed through the Father, Son, and the Holy Spirit. God has revealed Himself as Father, Son and Holy Spirit in Scripture, which are the three dimensions to His relationship with us. The doctrine of the Trinity doesn't adequately encapsulate the mysteries of God, but it's what our human minds can attempt to understand.

In the chapters ahead we will see the story of God raising "princes from the ashes" through His extravagant love—first as a Father who has adopted sons and daughters into His family, secondly as a Son who reigns as King and has called us to reign with Him, and thirdly as Holy Spirit who dwells in us as His abiding deposit of heavenly realities.

You can know the love of the Father. God is the creator of family and is the ideal Father. In a world of brokenness and distrust, we encounter the goodness of God as our Father. God has described His rescue story in terms of adopting us as His children. He rescued orphans and adopted them into His family.

You can know the love of the Son. God is the perfect Son. He gives us a glimpse of what His family is like, and He describes it as a Kingdom. His rescue story takes us from slavery into freedom as co-heirs in a Kingdom.

You can know the love of the Holy Spirit. God is the Holy Spirit. God has been actively working on the earth through His Holy Spirit since the very beginning. The gospel tells a scandalous rescue story of God taking us from a place where we were worthy of death to being made worthy to host God's Spirit.

I hope that the Church will be awakened in a fresh way to live out what Christ purchased for us—that the Church would look more and more like the pure and spotless Bride that Christ will return for. As Dietrich Bonhoeffer wrote, "They wander the earth and live in heaven, and although they are weak, they protect the world; they taste of peace in the midst of turmoil; they are poor, and yet they have all they want. They stand in suffering and remain in joy, they appear dead to all outward sense and lead a life of faith within." [2]

Love of the Father

CHAPTER ONE

Encountering a Truly Good Father

Kids eventually have to learn about the ways of life—the birds and the bees. I remember one time my oldest daughter, seven years old at the time, seemingly out of the blue, stating, "Everyone has a mother, but everyone does not have a father." My wife and I knew we had talked about this before, but as it often is with kids, we had to take time again to explain that biologically everyone has a mother and a father. Not everyone has a father and mother present in their lives, but everyone is brought into this world because of a father and a mother. It's the basic order of things that God set in motion.

The truth is, not everyone has had a good father in their life. And some haven't had a father in their life at all. And even for those who have had the blessing of a good father in their life, no one has a perfectly good father. In that sense, no one has an earthly father who is truly good. At this stage in life, with four young kids in the house, I am frequently reminded of the fact that I am not a perfect father. I long to be a good dad, but I sure know that I am not truly good. For that, we look to our Heavenly Father.

What is the answer for a generation jaded by the breakdown of the nuclear family? How do we begin to make sense of the brokenness around us resulting from instability, insecurity, and lack of commitment? Can we truly belong?

In Scripture, God describes Himself as Father to demonstrate that He is not only creator God (procreator of ones who bear His image), He is also provider and protector. Genesis 1:26 says, "Then God said, 'Let us make man in our image, after our likeness. And let them have dominion over the fish of the sea and over the birds of the heavens and over the livestock and over all the earth and over every creeping thing that creeps on the earth.'" He is the giver of life, but He is also meant to be our provider and keeper.

The problem is, early on in our story, we rebelled. That's right; we have all chosen our own way of being self-providers and self-protectors. Like adolescents who think they understand the world, we rebel from God, trying to make a way for ourselves. We can never escape from the reality that we didn't create ourselves, but for some reason we try to fool ourselves into thinking we can be our own protectors and providers.

THE WRETCHEDNESS OF THE ASHES

In a cold, drab, depressing cell at a youth detention center in the Olympic Northwest, I met a young girl named Sarah. Sarah met with me and another volunteer to talk about life and faith (and to have a break from her mundane life in a detention center). Sarah was only thirteen years old but was already jaded by the harsh realities of a broken world.

Sarah had always been on the run. Her single father was verbally and physically abusive. In elementary school, she realized she could find some respite on her friends' couches. From then on, she rarely went home to her father. Why would she? But it was only a matter of time before her attempts to survive on her own resulted in deeper trouble.

With her orphan spirit fully alive, she resorted to stealing and lying, just to survive. She started getting in trouble with the law at the age of eleven. The system didn't have answers for her or have a place for her. Between couch-surfing and teen homes, she wandered. Eventually, her involvement in a robbery landed her in the detention center.

Over a period of several weeks, another volunteer and I met with Sarah during our weekly visits to the center. We were a listening ear and a voice of encouragement. In one conversation, I felt led to share Psalm 113 with Sarah. God is, "the God who lifts us up from the ashes and props us up with princes." He is the Father she never had and the Father she always longed for. The extravagance of God's love in that moment was so evident to Sarah because of the stark realities of her life experiences. It was so clear to her that her life was a mess. While it wasn't all due to her own actions, she definitely hadn't been able to help herself.

This was one of the moments—the beautiful moments—where God calls and adopts one of His kids. This was the moment Sarah surrendered her life. She came running back to her Heavenly Father and began to trust Him with her life.

Sarah's story may seem more desperately cut and dry than some. She was obviously in need of something bigger than herself. But I tell that story because, in general, Sarah's story is no different than any of ours. Out on our own, without our Father, the world is a cold, dark, and lonely place. I believe we need to first have a revelation of where we were when God pursued us. He didn't forgive anyone who didn't need forgiving. He didn't redeem those who were already on their way to a pretty good life. No, He forgave the otherwise unforgivable and redeemed the irredeemable, which is every single one of us.

In his book *Why I am a Christian*, John Stott uses an old metaphor for God as "The Hound of Heaven" to describe the grace of God to encounter Him in the depths of the ashes. He says,

> It is due to Jesus Christ himself, who
> pursued me relentlessly even when I was

> running away from him in order to go
> my own way. And if it were not for the
> gracious pursuit of the Hound of Heav-
> en I would today be on the scrapheap of
> wasted and discarded lives. [3]

This Good Father I describe is the one who lifts us up from the ash heap (Ps. 113:7). He didn't grab the people who already were cleaned up and ready for adoption. No, He chose to adopt as His own sons and daughters who didn't want Him, who had actually rejected Him before that moment.

THE EXTRAVAGANCE OF GOD'S GRACE

God's extravagant and radical love shines all the more brilliantly when we know what He did to save us. It's hard to think of a more extreme depiction of the chasm that God reached across to save us than the story of the prophet Hosea in the Old Testament.

God uses this man of God to demonstrate the immensity of His love for Israel by asking Hosea to marry a prostitute. That's right, a prostitute. The Lord spoke to Hosea and said, "Go and marry a prostitute, so that some of her children will be conceived in prostitution. This will illustrate how Israel has acted like a prostitute by turning against the Lord and worshiping other gods" (Hos. 1:2, NLT). God tells us why He asks Hosea to do this crazy act. He wants to illustrate the unfaithfulness of Israel and contrast it with His perfect love.

Let it be clearly understood, the love of God is not what we were looking for. We chose other things and turned from our Father. We felt that we could do better on our own. We have the same independent spirit as Gomer the prostitute. In the story, Gomer runs away from Hosea and reverts to her old way of life. She continues sleeping around and chasing after other men. And this is what God reached into. Our ashes are not innocent. In Hosea 2:14-15 (NLT) ,God says,

> But then I will win her back once again.
>   I will lead her into the desert
>   and speak tenderly to her there.
> I will return her vineyards to her and
>   transform the Valley of Trouble into
>   a gateway of hope.
> She will give herself to me there,
>   as she did long ago when she was
>   young, when I freed her from her

captivity in Egypt.

This is God's plan. He's foretells how He will win back the heart of Israel and ultimately the heart of every human that will humble themselves. He will find us in the desert in the "Valley of Trouble".

God tells Hosea, "Go and love your wife again, even though she commits adultery with another lover. This will illustrate that the Lord still loves Israel, even though the people have turned to other gods and love to worship them" (Hos. 3:1, NLT).

We don't like this description of our condition. It's painful to look in the mirror of God's Word and realize how desperately we need God. Without Him we are a mess.

A FATHERLESS GENERATION

Over the last fifty years, we have heard about the impact and fallout incurred by a rise in fatherlessness in America. The presence of a father and stability of the home is one of the greatest determining factors for a child's success in academics, behavior, career, and society in general. As of 2016, 85% of all children that exhibit behavioral disorders, 71%

of all high school dropouts, and finally 63% of all teen suicides came from fatherless homes. [4]

The impacts of absent fathers are real and grave. But think of this as an illustration of who we are without Christ. Before we encounter the love of God, we are spiritual orphans, willingly fatherless. I often wonder how much of the world's pain is caused purely as a result of broken people hurting other broken people. We hurt people, who are themselves hurting others, and find ourselves in a heap of a mess. The King James Version of Psalm 113:7 translates the ash heap as "the dung hill." He lifts us out of the dung hill. We were stuck in the horrendous mess and smell of our own making.

Our fatherlessness is a result of our stubborn choice to try to protect and provide for ourselves. But this act of rebellion results in more innumerable messes that we can never fix.

LIKE NO OTHER

Jesus extended an invitation for us to encounter our perfect Heavenly Father. Jesus said, "If you knew me, you would also know my Father" (John 8:19, NLT). Jesus made it possible for us to be reunited with the Father, who not only created us in His image, but who is also our protector and provider.

Our Heavenly Father is the father we have been longing for. Our orphan spirit will never be content or secure in the love of anyone else. Father God truly is matchless. Where earthly fathers are impatient, He is always patient. Where fathers are unpredictable, He never changes. Where we know the shame of disappointing our fathers, our Heavenly Father still pursues us in our mistakes.

This is one of the core identities central to the gospel—our identity as a child of God. We have been adopted by the Father into the family of God. There's no need to keep running, striving, or fighting for our survival alone. We can find peace, rest, and love in God's family. This is the first dimension of God's love we will unpack. As Brennan Manning wrote, "The self-acceptance that flows from embracing core identity as Abba's child enables me to encounter my utter brokenness with uncompromising honesty and complete abandon to the mercy of God." [5]

CHAPTER TWO

The Relentless Father

Jesus said, "You therefore must be perfect, as your Heavenly Father is perfect" (Matt. 5:48). The Father is the standard for His kids. This means we must first come to know God as the perfect Father that He is if we are going to emulate Him.

I am so thankful for the life and example I've had in my earthly father. He encountered serious trials, yet he has remained faithful to Jesus. My dad's example of faith in the midst of tragedy was one of the driving influences in me surrendering my life to Jesus.

My parents were high school sweethearts. They came to know Jesus their senior year of high school. My mom first heard the gospel and shared it with my dad. These conversations and decisions will have an impact for generations to come. But as our family grew, my mom began to struggle with depression and eventually substance abuse. Her life began to spiral out of control and became more and more desperate.

Our home life grew more chaotic and confusing. After a few years of this battle with depression, it eventually ended with my mom taking her own life. I still remember that day—it's forever etched in my mind. I was called out of my first-grade classroom to come to the counselor's office, where my dad sat with a close family friend and the counselor. The brief explanation of what my mom did the night before was drowned out in my head by the deafening pain of loss and the unbelief of what was happening.

A BREACH OF TRUST

Every one of us experiences a breach of trust in this world. We are going along in life, naively thinking that things are going to be happily ever after, and then we hit it; we are met with the painful realities of sin, brokenness, selfishness, and destruction that have tormented humanity for millennia. Eventually we come face to face with the reality that everything is not alright in this world.

That moment in our lives—when we realize that there is pain in this world—can leave wounds that never go away. We sense that trust was broken. Everything was supposed be alright. Life was supposed to be a fairytale of sorts.

Trust is the basis of any relationship. People have always said, "Everything is going to be alright." Everything has not been alright. In fact, everything has been quite painful and difficult. Before we encounter the only Being that is perfect, we are helplessly caught in this trap of survival and growing cynicism. From that place, what can be trusted? Everything seems so fragile, so uncertain.

Everything changes when we see God for who He is and begin to see the tragedies of our lives in the radiant light of who He is. In that place, nothing else matters. In that moment, the pains feel so temporary because we finally realize the life-long desire for something to be certain. We have finally discovered the one thing our hearts have longed for—certainty. God is the essence and embodiment of certainty. He is the One who is called Faithful and True.

Tozer describes it like this,

> Here we acknowledge the essential unity of God's nature, the timeless persistence of His changeless being throughout eternity and time... If we grope back to the farthest limits of thought where imagination touches the pre-creation void, we shall find God there. In one unified present glance He comprehends all things from everlasting, and the flutter of a seraph's wing a thousand ages hence is seen by Him now without moving His eyes. [6]

THE FATHER'S PERFECTION

God's perfection is one of the most settling and assuring revelations to grapple with. We can be certain that there will be uncertainties. We don't know what tomorrow will bring. And beyond that, the only certainty we can know is the certainty of

God. This is the God of all things, who has revealed Himself and declared emphatically that of everything in the universe and Heaven, He is truly holy.

Holy literally means "wholly other" or set apart.[7] There's no comparison; He is matchless. It's an abrupt encounter that occurs when needy, restless orphans meet their perfect creator, and their entire lives are recalibrated as a result.

Moses was a man of uncertainties. Even though he is raised as royalty in Egypt, he comes to realize his origin story. The injustice he sees—his people enslaved by Egypt—compels him to action. Moses' own bad decisions and anger drive him to flee Egypt and everything he has known. That's where God reveals Himself as the "I Am." Speaking to Moses and piercing his orphan heart, God reassures Moses that in this cold, harsh, lonely world, on a countryside herding sheep, "I am Who I am" (Exodus 3:14). Moses can finally rest assured that God is not fickle or changing. He was, and is, and is to come—the only true certainty in the universe.

In Revelation 4:8, we see this picture of Heaven, "And the four living creatures, each of them with six wings, are full of eyes all around and within, and day and night they never cease to say, 'Holy, holy, holy, is the Lord God Almighty, who was and is and is to come!'"

God has always been holy, in need of no one. Any created being that looks upon Him, can't help but cry out about His perfection. It's so radiantly beautiful and "wholly other." This is the perfect One who has chosen to pursue us. Hebrews 7:26 says, "For it was indeed fitting that we should have such a high priest, holy, innocent, unstained, separated from sinners, and exalted above the heavens."

The perfect Father invites us into a relationship with Himself that our hearts have always wanted and needed. It's a relationship of certainty that can be trusted. James 1:17-18 says, "Every good gift and every perfect gift is from above, coming down from the Father of lights, with whom there is no variation or shadow due to change." We finally come to know a Father, in whom there is no shadow or variation.

Growing up, one question that my dad would often pose as I wrestled through hesitation or decision-making was, "What's the worst that can happen?" It was a practical question that walked me back from the cliff and helped me think rationally. But, deep down, I believe one reason I didn't receive his wisdom as trite or unfeeling was that I had watched my dad walk through difficulty and survive. In fact, I had watched him be refined and walk more in love with God, despite difficulties.

My dad's wisdom carried weight in my life because I knew it had been tested in the fire. If I can trust my earthly father, who is not perfect, I can trust my Heavenly Father who is the only being in the universe that is truly perfect. If the pain of my earthly father reveals an integrity that can be trusted, then my Heavenly Father has shown a trustworthiness beyond comprehension by willingly laying down His own life to pursue me. His pain was a different level of pain than the pain we can know—it's the willing pain of love, sacrificially endured to make a way. Our Father's character has been revealed to all humanity through the man Jesus Christ, who hung on the cross for you and me.

CONTRIBUTING TO THE MESS

It's settled that God is perfect and there is no other. And within His perfection is the extravagance of both His goodness and His justice. It's because He is perfect that He is so good. And it's because He is perfect that He is also just. As C.S. Lewis said, "Goodness is either the great safety or the great danger - according to the way you react to it." [8]

In this painful world, we can easily be fooled into thinking we are innocent. This sort of victimhood is at the root of an orphan spirit. A spiritual orphan thinks of themselves as relatively good, and therefore the pain they have faced is the result of others. But this is self-deception.

Early on in life, our trust was breached. Because of that brokenness, we recognize the only fully trustworthy One, our Heavenly Father. But as we peer into His perfection and flawless trustworthiness, we see that we have not been completely innocent victims in our lives. We realize that we ourselves have contributed to the chaos of humanity.

Growing up in a large family with seven kids, I took on the role of peacemaker and obedient child. I preferred to lay low and stay out of trouble. I thought if I could just do what I was told and stay quiet, maybe I could survive. I had one stepbrother who would resentfully call me "Mr. Perfect." Our house had a lot of loud personalities, arguing, and even fighting at times. But I just tried to avoid it all.

Being an obedient peacemaker can be good, but outside of a relationship with the Father, it can easily be a place to hide, and a breeding ground for passivity and arrogance. An orphan's attitude is, 'I have it figured out and I'll take care of myself.' Over time I began to grow a spirit of judgementalism and arrogance, resenting other people's behavior. Instead of compassion or mercy, I carried more pride. Even regarding my own mom's suicide, I remember thinking about the selfishness of her decision and resenting her for it. I remember beginning to embrace that spirit of an orphan which pretends that I am the innocent victim and everyone else is the problem.

Deep down, an orphan knows they are not perfect. I always knew that about myself, but a self-deception seeped into my heart, convincing me that I was not as bad as the others. I compared myself to others rather than the holiness of God. The truth is, I have contributed to brokenness in this world. In my own family, I contributed to the messiness of it all. Rather than an innocent orphan, a better description of each of us before meeting our Heavenly Father is a rebellious prodigal son or daughter.

THE RELENTLESS FATHER

The story in Luke 15 of the father and his two sons is etched in my mind. Jesus tells first century Jewish listeners of a young son demanding his inheritance prematurely. The entitled, naive young man goes off and squanders his inheritance and finds himself literally in a dunghill with pigs. After a little while, the young man has a moment of clarity and decides to return home and beg for mercy. Perhaps his father will allow him to be a servant on his estate.

Every fall semester, my college pastor would preach from that passage. It was his way of calling students to their Heavenly Father. He read the story and shared his own testimony and made a call for students to follow Jesus.

Inevitably he got to Luke 15:20, and, with tears running down his face, he read, "But while he was still a long way off, his father saw him and felt compassion, and ran and embraced him and kissed him." He shed tears every time, spoken as though he had just experienced it all over again.

The older son remained with his father. He remained and worked the estate but not necessarily with pure motives. When the younger son returns, it leaves the older resentful and jealous. He complains to his father, but his father conveys love to the older brother he never knew was his all along.

My college years were so transformative because of relationships like the one with my college pastor. Pastor Brad patiently sat with me, cried with me, prayed with me through stupidity and difficulty, and demonstrated the love of the Father in tangible ways. It was like the Father was giving me the opportunity to hear a sermon and see a sermon repeated for four years.

God's love is relentless. The story of these two sons in Luke 15 is about the Father's love for me. I was the younger son whom God lifted up from the ash heap, embraced, and accepted into the family. I needed a living encounter with His goodness that transcended all my historical wounds. But I was also the older brother who, in judgementalism, resented his little brother. It's impossible to live as a son when I am constantly comparing myself to others. A son is secure in His Father. A son lives to please the Father.

We are invited into a lifelong journey of experiencing the Father's love that we won't find anywhere else. It's perfectly good and it's perfectly just. It can be trusted. At times it can feel too immense, or we can be held back by shame or unbelief. But I promise that those who press in to know the Father's love will find the perfect Father they have always wanted to know.

CHAPTER THREE

Adopted

Romans 8:15
"For you did not receive the spirit of slavery to fall back into fear, but you have received the Spirit of adoption as sons, by whom we cry, 'Abba! Father!'"

One day, Jesus walked into the city of Jericho (Luke 19). Jesus's fame was beginning to spread, and crowds flocked to Him. They wanted to catch a glimpse of this miracle worker and great teacher. The people had heard about Him, and they wondered who He could be.

In the midst of the noise and the bustle, please know that Jesus is always watching. He is looking for a heart to turn to Him. He's looking to do it again—to lift the needy from the ash heap. This day Jesus didn't have to look down; instead, He looked up to find a man who had climbed up into a tree to catch a glimpse of Jesus. Jesus looked at this man, and although He had never met him, He already knew his name. He said to him, "Zacchaeus, today salvation has come to your house."

Zacchaeus was not used to belonging anywhere. He was wealthy and powerful because he had chosen a life of defrauding his neighbors and skimming from the top. He was scorned by the people of Jericho and had developed an attitude that life is better lived alone. But the air in Jericho was different this day. The Holy Spirit drew Zacchaeus from his normal work to come and catch a glimpse of this man everyone was talking about. Jesus chose Zacchaeus this day and gave him the opportunity to experience the salvation of the Kingdom. He called him to leave his life as a wandering orphan and be adopted into the family of God.

THE ORPHAN SPIRIT

In prior chapters we began to unpack the orphan spirit we are born into. This mindset is a worldview of independence, self-sufficiency, and selfishness. It's important to understand what Jesus saves us from. Properly understanding this saving work in our lives launches us into a life of relationship, purpose, and authority.

This revelation of transformation compelled Paul to write to the church in Rome and explain to them in Romans 8 the realities of this new life in Christ. He saved us from our independent orphan state and adopted us as sons and daughters. Jesus didn't save some people who were already pretty good and just make them better. He wasn't introducing His religion. He was adopting children into His family—a family that reigns together in a Kingdom (we will talk more about that in the next chapter). These kids were rebellious orphans and were adopted at a high price. God gave each of them an inheritance and place to belong.

In Jack Frost's book, *Spiritual Slavery to Spiritual Sonship*, he lays out a list of descriptors for an orphan. These can be helpful identifiers of the spirit

that causes havoc in our lives. To summarize, he
states:

1) To an orphan, God is not just Master
   but also taskmaster.
2) Orphans are independent and self-re-
   liant because they are convinced that
   they cannot trust anyone else.
3) Orphans value obedience over relationship.
4) Orphans are insecure but usually quite
   good at covering their insecurity.
5) Orphans are addicted to, and strive
   for the praise, approval, and acceptance of other people.
6) Orphans have shut off their hearts
   from love expressed on a deep
   level and therefore seek for comfort in
   counterfeits, such as addiction, com-
   pulsion, escapism, busyness, or hy-
   per-religious activity. [9]

Long gone are the days where we have to fight to
survive in loneliness and isolation. Addiction and
mindless busyness are part of our old way of life.
God has adopted us into His family. Now we belong in the Father. He picked us up from the ash
heap, dusted us off with the cleansing power of Je-

sus, and adopted us as children of His own.

THE SPIRIT OF ADOPTION

Paul describes the mysteries of God's redemption with the phrase "the Spirit of adoption" (Romans 8:15). The Father adopts us as children through the Holy Spirit. As Paul writes about salvation, he uses the Roman concept of adoption to illustrate the radical nature of God's work in our lives. In Roman law, adoption did not just affect civil status, it also gave the chosen heir rights, privileges, property, and responsibilities. This unique understanding of adoption is not found in Jewish or Greek culture but is peculiar to Roman culture. And yet, this is the description Paul uses to describe the miraculous transaction that takes place in salvation.

The spirit of adoption is the transactional miracle that takes place at salvation. And this miracle places upon the children of God rights, privileges, inheritance, and responsibilities. People can talk about becoming a Christian or making a decision to follow Jesus in terms that are rather casual. It can often be similar to changing your social media status or simply rearranging your schedule to fit in a few more religious activities. But this does not reflect the reality of what's taken place.

When Jesus talks about being "born again," He refers to the transaction of our orphan (or dormant) spirit being brought to life by the Holy Spirit. That moment marks the beginning of our life in the family of God. We no longer need to worry about our origin story because that is fixed in Christ. We no longer need to worry about our shame or the past; our Father took care of that.

THE POWER OF TRUE BELONGING

Jesus is our model for living as children of God. While Jesus walked the earth, He demonstrated how to live as children, submitted to and loved by the Father. There is no question about the motivation of Jesus's life. His one care was to be in tune with the Father's timing, the Father's business, the Father's values, the Father's agenda, and the Father's words.

Just consider one example at the beginning of Jesus's public ministry. In Matthew 3, Jesus is recognized as the Messiah by His forerunner and cousin, John the Baptist. John, somewhat reluctantly, baptizes Jesus in water. When Jesus comes out of the water, a voice from Heaven is heard saying, "This is my Son, in whom I am well pleased." Jesus is affirmed by John, but the only real affirmation He needs is the affirmation of His Father. He was publicly affirmed for all to hear.

This event inaugurates Jesus into public ministry. John falls to the background, and word begins to spread about Jesus. But Jesus is not interested in fame or popularity. He is only concerned with submitting to the Father's will. He is resolved in that because He is firmly secured in affirmation He has from the Father. That's the only thing that matters. And, unexpectedly, Jesus is led to the wilderness for forty days. There's no campaign or public promotional strategy to prepare the way for His ministry. He trusts and knows the Father.

There is such security in belonging. Our current age is filled with a chronic and epidemic sense of loneliness, isolation, and insecurity. This is not circumstantial or a result of our times being more chaotic than other times in history. In fact, we live in the most prosperous time in human history. We have more opportunities for mobility in every regard, and we are more technically connected than in any time in human history. Yet humans feel more alone and anxious than ever before. We need an awakening of the true gospel that calls sons and daughters back to their Father. Our hearts long for that place of belonging.

LIVING IN THE GOSPEL OF ADOPTION

So then, living in this gospel of adoption is the privilege and calling upon every follower of Jesus. Shame has no place in my life anymore. I am no longer an orphan. I'm not defined by my past; instead, I'm defined by Who I belong to. He has been writing a new story over my life. He found me in a pit, dirtied and beaten up by my own stupidity. He gave me value, picked me up out of the pit, cleaned me off, embraced me, and adopted me into His family. This transforms everything for me now.

Adoption is a change in relationship. We didn't belong, but now we do. We get to walk in relationship with our Father, in increasing measure. Jesus described our purpose in John 17:3 as He prayed to the Father. He said, "And this is eternal life, that they know you, the only true God, and Jesus Christ whom you have sent." We now have direct access to the Father and can talk with Him as Jesus talked with the Father while on Earth.

Jesus points us to that coming day when He says in John 14:16-17 "I will ask the Father, and He will give you another Helper, to be with you forever, even the Spirit of truth, whom the world cannot receive, because it neither sees him nor knows him. You know Him, for He dwells with you and will be in you. I will not leave you as orphans; I will come to you." We can call the Father "Abba" from this place of adoption. "Abba" is an Aramaic word Jesus used to refer to the Father. It reflects intimacy and affection. In some of His most horrific and difficult moments, Jesus cried out, "Abba!" That was His way of talking to Father in family terms. Just like some call their father "dad" or "papa." We have been given direct relationship with the Father and can call to Him like Jesus did.

Unfortunately, the Christian message is sometimes misunderstood as an instant transformation. We promote testimonies of success and turnaround, freedom from addictions, instant healings, job success, and quick financial provision. This emphasis, to the neglect of the everyday graces and miracles, can actually draw us away from the relationship that the Father brought us into. He adopted us into His family and filled us with the Spirit of adoption, so we can now call out "Abba, Father." We were brought into a relationship with our Heavenly Father, similar to the relationship that Jesus had while on Earth. This is an *everyday* miracle that we can walk in.

My life has been marked both by moments of instant change and by slow evolution over time. Both are beautiful expressions of my relationship with a powerful, loving God. He displays His raw strength through radical encounters that change me. He also demonstrates His eternal love that desires gradual, willful change in my heart, not just outward change. I am a completely different person than I was twenty-five years ago. But to pretend that all of that change was instant would take away from the beauty of the long journey of my relationship with my Father. Transformation that has led me from glory to glory and which is not complete yet points to a story of God rescuing me from the ashes and lifting me up to live in the heights of the places He's destined me to live.

Through Jesus, the Father restores the order He first intended. He calls back His sons and daughters. Francis Schaefer describes this renewal of things, "But the Bible declares, and it should be joy to us, that when I have accepted Christ as my

Savior, I immediately come into a new relationship with the Father, and I become his son, in the sense of the creature in the proper place for which he was made in the first place." [10]

We are made with a purpose. When we encounter our Father, we come to understand that we are not an accident—a random assortment of cells and experiences—but a created being, put here on purpose with a purpose. The gospel imagery for understanding this purpose is the adoption as sons.

Now in this highly polarized and politically correct age, the emphasis on sons over daughters may be alienating to some. But as Jack Frost insists, in the age to come, the Bible tells us we will all be living as the Bride of Christ, so it will get equaled out, in time. All joking aside, Paul is describing this transaction to the first century church. In first century Rome, inheritance was transferred to sons, not to daughters. Therefore, this is good news to men and women alike. This means we are all adopted as sons into the family, with authority, inheritance, rights, and privileges. That is not a gender statement, that is a statement of equally good news for all.

For as Paul stated earlier in Galatians, "But now

that faith has come, we are no longer under a guardian, for in Christ Jesus you are all sons of God, through faith. For as many of you as were baptized into Christ have put on Christ. There is neither Jew nor Greek, there is neither slave nor free, there is no male and female, for you are all one in Christ Jesus. And if you are Christ's, then you are Abraham's offspring, heirs according to promise" (Gal. 3:25-29). Men and women alike are called sons in the family of God. That is not a de-valuing of women but, in fact, a valuing of women. In a culture where women had very limited rights and privileges, Paul is making clear the radical nature of the gospel that Jesus demonstrated through His life to call women as well as men. And this call comes with the full rights and privileges, male and female, Jew and Greek, free and slave.

Where the orphan is insecure and codependent, the adopted child of God is confident in their place of belonging in the family. A child of God does not have to be swayed by everyone's opinion of them. They seek to please their Father and be about their Father's business. Their need for people is tied to their need to grow in Christlikeness and selflessness; it is not tied to a need for value, worth, and belonging in the eyes of others.

In the Luke 15 story of the prodigal son, when the father is reunited with his son, he puts a ring on his finger. In first century near-eastern culture, a ring was a tool for carrying out family business. The ring could be a signet ring to seal documents and grant signatory authority for transactions. The father was granting his son that authority to be about the family business again. God lifts us out of the shame of our stupidity and places an authority upon our lives.

Our Heavenly Father has placed a ring on your finger. His adoption of you is not into a generic place of spectating. Instead, He expects His children "to be about the Father's business." It's the privilege of His children to be about the family business. He entrusted us to represent Him and to point people to Him.

RIDE THE WAVE

I had an amazing experience with the Lord a few years back. I was privileged to be part of ministry that God was doing in other areas of the country. While on these trips, God surprised me by speaking a repeated message to me through multiple voices. My first trip was to southern California as part of a twenty-one-day school equipping young people in different spheres of media. It was an amazing atmosphere of faith, energy, and creativity. At one point, my friend and I snuck in the back of a breakout session on the topic of publicly proclaiming the gospel. The facilitator was wrapping up the session when he changed course and called me out from the back of the room. He said, "We have a guest in the room, and I want us to pray over him." He was pointing to me, and before I knew it, about thirty young adults gathered around me and began to pray. Several significant words and prayers were spoken over me, but one word specifically stood out and began reoccurring over the next several months. The young lady said, "I see you surfing on a wave. You are free. You are full of joy. And it's the power of the wave carrying you and propelling you forward." It was clear that God was giving me a picture of what it looks like to live as a child of God.

A few months later, I was traveling again, this time with my family, visiting northern California. We have some friends in Redding, and appreciate the opportunity to worship at Bethel Church, so we stopped by for a few days. One of our friends, who is a teacher in Bethel's middle school, invited us to come visit her classroom. It was fun to see how they facilitated that environment for even younger people. But then she asked if her class could pray over us. These kids obviously knew God and were mature beyond their years in prayer. But again, one word carried the same theme as a few months prior. The young child said, "I see Drew surfing on a wave. He caught the wave and is filled with the joy of riding the wave." Again, it was the vivid picture of the God-confidence available to the children of God.

Within a few months, I was thrown into new leadership challenges and at times felt in over my head. That temptation to strive and try harder was creeping into my mind and heart. One Sunday, after the morning worship service, a family from our church grabbed my attention and wanted to encourage me. The husband said, "While you were speaking this morning, I saw this vivid picture of you surfing on a wave. I feel like you've stepped into an authority in Christ. And I want to encourage you to enjoy the ride." That repeated word touched my heart, and I felt the Father's affection all over again. I knew that the best and freest place I can be is resting in the authority that Jesus purchased for me as child of God. I belong, and He adopted me with a high

price. It's my honor to enjoy the ride as His power
propels me forward.

Responding to the Love of the Father

We have all found ourselves in a "pit" or "ash heap" at some point in our lives. The depth and range of the "ash heap" varies from person to person, but we've all found ourselves there. What has the "ash heap" looked like in your life?

When the Father rescued you, how did you recognize His hand reaching out for you? Think about the specific events that took place and write them down.

Have you ever found yourself having a difficult time trust God as a perfectly good Father? Try to think about why that might be. Was there a time in your life when trust was broken? Stop right now and ask God to help you see and recognize any places where trust has been broken in your life. Ask Him to help heal those places.

Take time to declare that God is your perfect Father - that He is your provider and protector. Take time to confess doubts or unbeliefs. Allow Him to minister to you in this moment. Write down the truths that come into your mind and heart.

Have you ever struggled with having an "orphan spirit"? Look back at the characteristics of an orphan on page 42. Identify and underline those characteristics that have shown up in your life. Now ask God the Father if there are any of those characteristics that are still present.

Take time to thank God for the "Spirit of adoption." Meditate on the truth that you are adopted into the family and that you truly belong in Him. Think, pray, write out what it means to be part of a family.

Lastly, write out how your life would be different if you never struggled with having an "orphan spirit".

James 1:17
Every good gift and every perfect gift is from above, coming down from the Father of lights, with whom there is no variation or shadow due to change.

Luke 15:20
And he arose and came to his father. But while he was still a long way off, his father saw him and felt compassion, and ran and embraced him and kissed him.

Romans 8:15
For you did not receive the spirit of slavery to fall back into fear, but you have received the Spirit of adoption as sons, by whom we cry, "Abba! Father!"

John 17:3
And this is eternal life, that they might know you, the only true God, and Jesus Christ whom you have sent.

John 14:16-18

I will ask the Father, and He will give you another Helper, to be with you forever, even the Spirit of truth, whom the world cannot receive, because it neither sees him nor knows him. You know Him, for He dwells with you and will be in you. I will not leave you as orphans, but I will come to you.

Galatians 3:25-29

But now that faith has come, we are no longer under a guardian, for in Christ Jesus you are all sons of God, through faith. For as many of you as were baptized into Christ have put on Christ. There is neither Jew nor Greek, there is neither slave nor free, there is no male and female, for you are all one in Christ Jesus. And if you are Christ's, then you are Abraham's offspring, heirs according to promise.

Love of the Son

CHAPTER FOUR

Encountering the Son

Hebrew 12:28-29
"Therefore, let us be grateful for receiving a kingdom that cannot be shaken, and thus let us offer to God acceptable worship, with reverence and awe, for our God is a consuming fire."

Growing up in school, part of our education is learning about ancient civilizations. Everyone learns about Mesopotamia, the Egyptians, the Mayans, and others. These powerful civilizations still mark our world today with artifacts and architectural wonders. As much as we learn about the contributions and innovations of those cultures, we quickly learn that each of these civilizations not only rose to power, but also crumbled into the ash heap of history. Each of these kingdoms, empires, or civilizations have one thing in common: they came to an end.

In all their power, in all their strength, and military expansion, eventually these kingdoms came to an end. Now they are part of our history books. I once got the opportunity to visit the site of some of the tallest Mayan pyramids to be discovered in the rainforests of Guatemala. They are a beautiful sight to behold, and a testament to human ingenuity and innovation. One day, we climbed to the top of one of the pyramids and looked out over the rainforest. We saw a half dozen protruding hills standing above the tree line of the forest. My friend, who was hosting me, explained that archeologists believe each of those protruding hills also contain a pyramid that has yet to be uncovered. It struck me as ironic, that the power and beauty of a people could be so magnificent, but also be so quickly forgotten. Literally, the majesty of their age is now covered by dirt.

It puts the temporal nature of our age into perspective. Every kingdom assumes they will always be. Every culture has a myopic sense that they are invincible. Icons will be forgotten. Monuments will be torn down or deteriorate. History will be told and retold again, and even the retelling will evolve.

But one civilization has been revealed as an everlasting kingdom. The primary focus of Jesus's teaching was the Kingdom of Heaven. He spoke of the language, values, behaviors, and agenda of this Kingdom of Heaven.

God has revealed Himself to us, not just as Father, but also as Son. God is Son. He is the One who rules and reigns, creates and leads with all authority and sovereign wisdom. And the Son came and lived as Jesus—the God-man, born of a woman and by the Holy Spirit. He came to Earth and introduced to us a Kingdom from another world and invited us into it. He introduced a Kingdom that is unshakeable and is, in fact, eternal.

This understanding of being brought into a Kingdom is the basis for the second aspect of gospel identity. When we decide to follow Jesus, we must understand what it means to now be a part of a Kingdom.

BORING CHRISTIANITY?

Is it possible to follow the Son and be bored? People go to church for a variety of reasons, but for many, they can't argue with the reality that boredom is an accurate description of their life and faith. Is boredom compatible with the gospel? Is this gospel of the Kingdom that Jesus came to declare a call to a confining life of safety and boredom?

This modern boredom in Christianity is characterized by sleepy Sundays where people don't want their Christianity to follow them outside of the building. It's evidenced through doctrine being affirmed verbally, but not being lived out. People are excited about and devoted to sports and entertainment, but this is often missing for eternal matters.

I am more convinced than ever that the deficiency we see in church points to a shortcoming in us, not in God or His rescue story. Maybe the apathy or boredom we experience results from a lack of understanding (or should I say revelation) of the beautiful and inexhaustible nature of the love of God.

This points to the church's failure to emphasize

and articulate the rescue story of Heaven in a way that affects our entire life. A faith that's confined to a Sunday morning is not a faith at all. And one of the primary aspects of this failure of the church is a lack of emphasis on "Kingdom." The lens of God's story as a Kingdom invading the earth is an adventurous, risk-filled, raw, and radical story of God's love for us. He's waking us up to jump in and not hold back any part of our lives.

I'm confident that more and more individuals are being awakened to the stark difference between religious adherence and the Christianity of the Kingdom that impacts every facet of our life. This is a call to devotion and surrender. Are you ready?

THE PIT OF SLAVERY

He is the one who lifts the needy from the ash heap and places them with princes (Psalm 113:7-8). This is a miraculous leap from bondage to freedom. It's a transformation from slavery to ruling and reigning with Christ. We have to understand the depths from which He rescues us so we can more greatly appreciate the heights to which He positions us. As John Stott said, "It's only against the inky blackness of the night sky that the stars begin to appear, and it is only against the dark background of sin and judgement the gospel shines forth." [11] Let's catch a glimpse of the pit of slavery.

God has used the nation of Israel as a main player in His redemptive story. To this day, the people of Israel are God's people, and He uses them to reveal His plan of salvation to the earth. A thousand years before King Jesus was revealed, the people of Israel found themselves enslaved in Egypt. For almost four hundred years, God's people were subject to another kingdom, to another king's agenda and priorities. After four hundred years, enough time had passed that freedom became a distant memory. The only thing they knew was bondage to a cruel master. The rulers of Egypt were fascinated with the afterlife and thought of themselves as gods. They enslaved the Jewish people for one purpose: their own glory.

God intervenes on that backdrop. It's into this hopeless situation, in the pit of slavery, that God redeems and transforms. We read the Exodus story as real history, but we also read it as a foreshadowing of what is to come. A day of deliverance is approaching when the Messiah will come and miraculously rescue His children out of slavery. He wants them to return to being subject to one Lord.

On the Jewish New Moon festival and Israel's Independence Day, Jews still quote what is called "Hallel." Hallel is a recitation in Hebrew of Psalm 113 through Psalm 118. These six chapters of Psalms point to the depths of slavery in Egypt, God's miraculous rescue in the Exodus, revival in Israel, and worship. They read these Psalms and remind themselves that Yahweh rescued them from the ash heap of slavery in Egypt.

The context of our miraculous rescue was slavery. We had surrendered our will to the enemy and were enslaved to his priorities. We had lost our rights and ability to defend ourselves. We were subjects of a master other than our Creator. King Jesus redeems us out of a slavery of our own making. He places us as valued citizens in His Kingdom. It's an extravagant message of grace and transformation.

In the book of Romans, Paul uses the imagery of slavery to explain the depths of where we were before King Jesus. We are not inherently good. Instead, we are in bondage. He says, "Thank God! Once you were slaves of sin, but now you wholeheartedly obey this teaching we have given you.

Now you are free from your slavery to sin, and you have become slaves to righteous living. Because of the weakness of your human nature, I am using the illustration of slavery to help you understand all this. Previously, you let yourselves be slaves to impurity and lawlessness, which led ever deeper into sin. Now you must give yourselves to be slaves to righteous living so that you will become holy" (Rom. 6:17-19, NLT).

Ancient Roman slavery was different from slavery in Egypt or, more recently, the colonial chattel slavery that we are more familiar with. In Roman culture, individuals could surrender themselves to slavery to repay debt or as a more consistent source of labor. Roman slaves could even own land. There is willfulness to our slavery that it's important to acknowledge. While we did not have a choice being born into the curse, we chose—time and time again—the illusion of civility disguised in other masters. Slavery looks good for a time because we think there's assurance of sustenance or acceptance in this world. But, by the grace of God, the Holy Spirit opens our eyes to see the pit that is slavery. And Jesus is merciful to pull us out.

THE EXTRAVAGANCE OF ROYALTY

In C.S. Lewis's brilliant novel, *The Horse and His Boy*, Lewis tells the story about a boy named Shasta and his adventure to Narnia and the North. Shasta finds himself fleeing his master and meets unexpected friends along the way. He meets Bree the horse, who can talk and has always longed for his homeland, and he meets Aravis and her talking horse Hwin. It's an adventure of discovery and personal transformation, and at one point, Bree helps Shasta understand the impact of slavery on the human mind. He says, "But one of the worst results of being a slave and being forced to do things is that when there is no one to force you any more you find you have almost lost the power of forcing yourself." [12]

King Jesus granted us freedom. The journey ahead is about discovering the beauty and the heights of freedom in God. It's no longer a life of coercion, manipulation, and lies. For some, the gospel has been reduced to a tamed message about simply going to Heaven. But the heart of the gospel is God rescuing us from willful exile and placing us in positions of worth in a Kingdom. The values of true love and true willful freedom are of the highest order in this Kingdom.

The size of the chasm crossed by God's grace is not just because of the depths of our brokenness. It's such a great distance because of the heights of His Kingdom in which He positions us. This act of "placing us with princes" is the wondrous beauty of the gift of grace. We have the privilege of a lifetime and an eternity of discovering the riches of His grace.

Romans 6:18 (NLT) says, "Now you are free from your slavery to sin, and you have become slave to righteous living." We are no longer slaves, but subject to a new master, the good King Jesus. And He doesn't just let us into His Kingdom but appoints us as co-heirs in His Kingdom and calls us to rule and reign with Him. It is explained in Ephesians 2:4-7, "But God, being rich in mercy, because of the great love with which he loved us, even when we were dead in our trespasses, made us alive together with Christ—by grace you have been saved—and raised us up with him and seated us with him in the heavenly places in Christ Jesus, so that in the coming ages he might show the immeasurable riches of his grace in kindness toward us in Christ Jesus."

Christ raised us up from slavery and seated us with Him in heavenly places. Our born-again experience is a spiritual transaction where sons and daughters are brought out of slavery and into a position of authority in the Kingdom. This is the extravagance of God's grace. To understand this in greater measure is the privilege of every child of God.

A KINGDOM NOT A DEMOCRACY

The word that is translated "kingdom" is used more than eighty times in the New Testament. This is a major theme of the gospel, and critical to understanding what Christ is accomplishing on the earth. The Greek word "basileia" is translated as "kingdom" in English. The word has two principle meanings: 1) a king's rule, reign, dominion, or authority; and 2) the territory or people over whom a king reigns.[13] The focal point in each of these translations is the King.

In the West, and predominantly in the twenty-first century, we are familiar with democracies (the rule of the people) or constitutional republics. We aren't as familiar with monarchies or kingdoms. Western forms of government have built-in checks and balances that keep branches of power contained in their proper bounds. A kingdom is different. A kingdom has no checks and balances. A king has no bounds to his power or authority in his kingdom. In earthly terms, this form of government is similar to a dictatorship or a fascist state, where everything rests upon the character, integrity, and ability of a human king.

When we surrender our life to King Jesus, we are ushered into a Heavenly Kingdom. We have a place at the King's table. King Jesus doesn't have any checks or balances. He rules and reigns, perfectly and totally. This can seem alarming if we think in earthly terms, but this is good news. Even for Western-minded, twenty-first century believers, this is such good news. We now have a leader, who rules and calls the shots, and does so perfectly. The King's domain is better than any democracy.

I am writing this book in the midst of an election year in the United States. Every four years, each respective party gives a pitch that their leader will be the "savior" we need. The people get drawn into the riptide of political banter, and our hopes become fixed on a human leader being the answer for the issues we face.

We know deep down that no man or woman can lead perfectly. We know that a president can't singlehandedly fix a nation. Yet many either get pulled into despair at the thought of the opposing party's candidate or starry-eyed hopes for the future that resides in their own party's candidate. I'm not saying that politics don't serve a purpose or that they are unimportant. I'm saying that, at a fundamental level, we long to be led. This is why the good news is such good news. King Jesus is the perfect leader. He is above a need for a democracy. He doesn't need to be voted into office. He doesn't need a confirmation hearing or a vote of approval. He is King, and it is such a freeing privilege to live life under the rule of King Jesus.

This is our new paradigm: the paradigm of a Kingdom. In the book of Revelation, the apostle John describes our future hope, and we see this theme played out clearly. He says of Jesus's followers who come out of the great tribulation, "Therefore they are before the throne of God, and serve Him day and night in His temple; and He who sits on the throne will shelter them with His presence. They shall hunger no more, neither thirst anymore; the sun shall not strike them, nor any scorching heat. For the Lamb in the midst of the throne will be their shepherd, and He will guide them to springs of living water, and God will wipe away every tear from their eyes" (Rev. 7:15-17). We are brought into this Kingdom, and it is our great privilege to learn to live under the rulership and authority of the One True King.

His Rule and His Will

For her eighth birthday, our daughter Luci had one request. She wanted her own room. She has two sisters and loves them dearly, but also dreamed of the day when she could have her own space. Of our four kids, Luci most appreciates her time alone. She likes to escape the noise of a loud household and be alone with her dolls and imagination.

So, Tanya and I decided to fulfill this birthday wish. We surprised her with a Paris-themed bedroom of her very own. My wife enjoyed finding Eiffel Tower decor and French antiques at local thrift stores. The space came together, and we surprised her with it a few days before her actual birthday. She loved it and quickly began to value the responsibility of having her own space. She was meticulous about keeping it clean. She loved spending time there and the feeling of independence.

One day Luci wanted to show me a new addition to her room. She had created a list of rules for her room. She decided if this was her space, then she would decide the rules there. At the top of list was "No boys allowed (except Dad)." Next, she declared "No food or drink (except water)." She continued on, "Clean up after yourself," and "No taking toys from room." She felt a rush of power from being the one who calls the shots. I'm sure it was freeing for her.

As humans, we love to call the shots. This is true both in positions of authority over others and in our own personal life. For Luci, she had authority over her domain. With authority comes the responsibility of setting the rules and expectations. We love to sit on the throne of our own heart.

All of that changes when we surrender to Jesus.

Salvation involves the removal of ourselves as king and welcoming King Jesus to His rightful place on the throne of our hearts. We no longer call the shots. We no longer set the rules. We admit that we don't know what's best. Instead, there is a perfect King who rules and reigns perfectly and is the most effective leader for our life.

THE PERFECT KING

Psalm 89:8 says, "O Lord God of hosts, who is mighty as you are, O Lord, with your faithfulness all around you?" The prophet Isaiah said, "For thus says the One who is high and lifted up, who inhabits eternity, whose name is Holy; 'I dwell in the high and holy place, and also with him who is of a contrite and lowly spirit, to revive the spirit of lowly, and to revive the heart of the contrite'" (Isa. 57:15). The apostle John refers to King Jesus coming with the name "Faithful and True" (Rev. 19:11). There's none like Him. He is above and unlike any ruler or master we can know on the earth.

A major aspect of walking with God is coming to know Him as King. Jesus is known as the Christ. This term literally means "Anointed" or "Anointed One" or even more directly "Messiah." In the early church, this became one of the most common ways to refer to Jesus, "Jesus the Christ." He is the fulfillment of prophetic Scripture that pointed to a Messiah from the royal line of David. The first verse of the Gospel of Matthew, says, "Jesus Christ, the Son of David." As His fame grew because of His miracles and teachings, the people said, "Can this be the Son of David?" (Matt. 12:23). He was regarded as King, representing the golden age of Israel.

David was regarded as the greatest earthly king of Israel. He was a national hero because he led Israel back to the priorities of God's presence and worship of the God of Israel, which resulted in a period of prosperity and favor. He gave them hope for the future. There would be One who would come as a descendant of David and would establish the Kingdom of God on Earth. As the prophet Daniel said, "I saw in the night visions, and behold, with the clouds of heaven, there came one like a son of man, and he came to the Ancient of Days and was presented before him. And to him was given dominion and glory and a kingdom, that all peoples, nations, and languages should serve him; his dominion is an everlasting dominion, which shall not pass away, and his kingdom one that shall not be destroyed" (Dan. 7:13-14).

Jesus was the King of Israel in the line of David, both in genealogy and legacy. And He came as the King of all kings, meaning not just the King of Israel but the King of all earthly rulers. As Revelation 1:5 describes Him, "Jesus Christ, the faithful witness, the firstborn of the dead, and the ruler of kings on earth." He revealed Himself as the King above all kings, rulers, and authorities on the earth.

The way of the Kingdom is freedom experienced through surrender. It's a paradox that we may hesitate to embrace. But because He is unlike anything in the universe and can be perfectly trusted, our surrender to Him is the safest place we can be. We must realize that we truly are not the best leader of our life and then trust this perfect King to have authority over our lives.

One day I sat in my office with a man who had made a mess of his life. He had gotten himself into financial and legal trouble, and his relationship with his fiancée was stuck in a downward spiral. As we talked through his story and how things got this bad, we finally got to the question that mattered most, "What are you going to do about it?" His answer was revealing. He said, "I'm going to get a second job. I'm going to get a good lawyer. And I'm going to ask my fiancée for forgiveness." In essence, he reflected the common human response of "I'm going to try harder."

This reaction reveals what we believe about ourselves and what we believe about true relationship with God. We are often blinded to the reality of our own powerlessness. We assume that if we just try harder, things will turn around. I ended up sharing with him the good news of Jesus, that freedom is found in surrender. We are able to cope with life's problems when we come to the end of our own abilities and fully surrender our life to Jesus. God is made strong in our weakness, and true Christianity is a life of surrender to a King that is perfect. I introduced him to the King.

This answer of surrender to the King doesn't instantly change our circumstances. All of this man's problems didn't just go away. But something more important happened. He finally stepped down from the throne of his heart and welcomed King Jesus to His rightful place. He stepped into the greatest place of freedom and submitted himself to the King of the universe. What Jesus said is true, "If anyone would come after me, let him deny himself and take up his cross and follow me. For whoever would save his life will lose it, but whoever loses his life for my sake and the gospel's will save it" (Mark 8:34-35).

INCREASED GOVERNMENT

The prophet Isaiah spoke about the Messiah to come seven hundred years before Jesus was born. He said,

> For to us a child is born, to us a son is given; and the government shall be upon his shoulder, and his name shall be called Wonderful Counselor, Mighty God, Everlasting Father, Prince of Peace. Of the increase of his government and of peace there will be no end, on the throne of David and over his kingdom, to establish it and to uphold it with justice and with righteousness from this time forth and forevermore. The zeal of the Lord of hosts will do this (Isa. 9:6-7).

He foretold the day of this King, or Prince of Peace coming and ruling "on the throne of David." He prophesied that a characteristic of His rule would be an increase in His government. He was coming to introduce a Kingdom that would be unshakable and ever increasing.

We are introduced into a Kingdom because of what Jesus started two thousand years ago, but He doesn't want us to stay at the gates of His Kingdom. He wants to increase King Jesus's rule in each of our lives. God is establishing a Kingdom in the hearts of people. It's not a kingdom of bricks and mortar, structures, and bureaucracies. And His plan is to increase his governmental rule in the hearts of His people.

For the three hundred years following Jesus's death and resurrection, Christianity spread like wildfire throughout the known world, even though it was a movement of the lower class and primarily uneducated. With ebbs and flows, it has continued to increase across the earth, until one day every tribe, tongue, and nation will hear (Rev. 7:9). In fact, the last century of Christianity has seen exponential growth in developing parts of the world, specifically in Africa and Asia.

But this increase is not on a global or historic scale. It's meant to be an increase in rule in each of our hearts individually. Peter was one of Jesus's closest disciples during His public ministry. Peter was zealous, devoted, faith-filled, and sometimes impulsive. But it's evident that King Jesus's rule was increasing in his life.

Peter was the first disciple to publicly and rightly declare that Jesus is, "the Messiah, the Son of the living God" (Matt. 16:16, NLT). Peter recognized Jesus as King, which meant Peter was willing to devote his life to following Him. But that confession didn't prevent Peter from making a common mistake. On the night of Jesus's arrest, Peter denies Jesus three times. Not once, not twice, but three times Peter denies knowing or being associated with King Jesus. What happened?

Peter climbed back on the throne of his own heart. Peter began to call the shots again. He was humiliated by his own flaky and timid response. Scripture says he "wept bitterly" (Matt. 26:75). He didn't realize how quickly he would kick King Jesus off the throne of his heart. But again, this is a story of God's extravagant grace. Following the resurrection, Peter, most likely sulking in self-pity and discouragement, had gone back to the life he knew as a fisherman. Jesus encounters Peter there once again. Three times, Jesus gives Peter an opportunity to return and again experience the grace of King Jesus's increasing rule in his life. Jesus restores Peter with the grace-filled command to "follow me" (John 21:19). King Jesus affirms the devotion He knows that Peter will demonstrate, and prophesies Peter's future martyrdom. Talk about an increase in the rule of King Jesus. Peter goes from denying Jesus before a little girl to giving his life as a martyr.

When we first surrender, we may assume that we have given King Jesus full access to every part of our heart. But as we walk with Him, we realize we haven't fully surrendered, and we're hanging on to things, clinging to comfort or control. Then we need that revelation of God's grace once again to meet us and call us to "follow me." Peter wasn't done growing after his encounter with the resurrected Christ. Peter surrendered his mouth and his leadership in his experience of baptism in the Holy Spirit in Acts 2, allowing God to use him in even greater ways. In Acts 10, Peter overcame the limits he had put on King Jesus ruling and reigning over his prejudices towards Gentiles. Truly God is calling us to go with Him from glory to glory, allowing His rule to increase in our lives.

What a privilege it is to follow King Jesus, who is full of grace and kindness, and calls us to further surrender. He sees more in us. He shows us our inheritance that sits dormant because of our lack of trust or desire for control. He positions us to be stretched so we finally let go of inhibitions and the fear of people's opinions. This is the life of Jesus's increased rule in our life. It's the call upon every follower of Jesus.

CHAPTER SIX

Life in the Kingdom

Galatians 5:1
"For freedom Christ has set us free; stand firm there-
fore, and do not submit again to a yoke of slavery."

Our eternal trajectory is towards a Kingdom. We live as citizens of a Kingdom now, but we also look forward to a greater fulfillment of that Kingdom in the age to come. We are living in the age of here, but not yet. We are living in the Kingdom that Jesus introduced here and now, but we recognize that the world around us is not yet made new. It's like we are caught between two worlds:

the internal living reality of King Jesus and the not-yet, future hope of the New Heaven and New Earth. This 'in between' is an opportunity to live as ambassadors. Our mission as representatives of a Kingdom is to declare that the Kingdom of God is near. We bring Jesus's hope and redemption. We see the world through a lens of eternity. We know the day is coming when "every knee will bow in heaven and on earth and under the earth - and every tongue will confess that Jesus Christ is Lord, to the glory of God the Father" (Phil. 2:10-11). All creation will see Him for Who He is.

This transforms the way we live because now every disfunction or broken situation becomes an invitation to redeem and renew. We no longer have to live hopelessly wringing our hands over worldly problems. We are now the most hope-filled people on the planet. This is because we have a personal hope in Jesus and also because we know where this story is going. We know that Jesus will make all things new with His redemptive plan.

Jesus's Church is a band of people fully convinced of who their King is and who they are in Him. They are not a dwindling group of mere survivors, but a growing Body of devoted followers of King Jesus

who understand what they are a part of. The Kingdom Church is the fulfillment of Paul's prayer in
Ephesians 1:18-23:

> Having the eyes of your hearts enlight-
> ened, that you may know what is the
> hope to which he has called you, what are
> the riches of his glorious inheritance in
> the saints, and what is the immeasurable
> greatness of his power toward us who
> believe, according to the working of his
> great might that he worked in Christ
> when he raised him from the dead and
> seated him at his right hand in the heav-
> enly places, far above all rule and author-
> ity and power and dominion, and above
> every name that is named, not only in
> this age but also in the one to come. And
> he put all things under his feet and gave
> him as head over all things to the church,
> which is his body, the fullness of him who
> fills all in all.

This is our new life of freedom in a Kingdom. Now
that we have stepped down from the throne of our
hearts and have devoted ourselves to King Jesus,
what do our daily lives look like? How do we han-

dle trials and difficulties? How does this new understanding of the gospel impact our relationship with God, our purpose in life, and our authority to fulfill all that God called us to?

It's not possible to live as citizens of the Kingdom of Heaven and continue to live like those in the world around us. I once heard it described in terms of taking a trip to a foreign land. Imagine you are taking a one-month trip to Paris, France. The city is so full of history, culture, and beauty. You plan on taking it all in—the sites, people, and experiences—but you know it's only temporary. You know that Paris is not your home. While you are there, you don't accumulate a bunch of trinkets and things that you cannot bring back home. Instead, you spend your money on things that will last—experiences and memories with people. You know your time is short there, so you desire to make the most of every day. As you talk with locals, you are not shy about where your home is. You take interest in the local culture and people, but don't try to morph into a local Parisian. You are a still a citizen of your home country, and you are not living like, nor seeking to become, a citizen of Paris.

We are citizens of the Kingdom of Heaven. That is

our home. We are foreigners, or visitors in another world. Too often, this message is neglected in the church. God's plan was to make us into "a kingdom of priests" (Rev. 1:6), and for us to be conscious of our Kingdom home. 2 Corinthians 5:9 says, "whether we are at home or away, we make it our aim to please Him." We live with an awareness of eternity and choose to live "by faith and not by sight" (2 Cor. 5:7).

This isn't always easy. There is a battle waging against a kingdom of darkness. We have been brought out of the kingdom of darkness and into the Kingdom of light, but the kingdom of darkness continues to rear its face in our lives. The kingdom of darkness is a spiritual kingdom with a real enemy. He engages in battle in different ways, and it's important that we understand this as a follower of King Jesus.

THE SPIRITUAL BATTLE

There is a real enemy. Satan, our accuser, has been actively at work on Earth from the beginning. I bring this to our attention not to stoke fear, but to stir awareness, vigilance, and courage. This is just another example of why life in the Kingdom cannot be seen as boring. God has entrusted us with a battle.

If we lack awareness of the enemy, or the reality of a spiritual battle, we can end up wrongly blaming God for the circumstances we face. God is sovereign and ultimately in control, but in His sovereignty, He has chosen to allow the enemy to work on the earth. We've seen this since the beginning in the garden of Eden, or in the life of Job. If we acknowledge the reality of a battle, we can respond to difficulties and trials with courage and faith, instead of discouragement and doubt.

There has always been resistance to God's rule and reign. The battle has always raged. That's why Paul encourages us to "Put on the whole armor of God, that you may be able to stand against the schemes of the devil" (Eph. 6:11). Our enemy wants to steal, kill, and destroy. We cannot be ignorant to that reality in this Kingdom. We need to trust King Jesus's power to crush the enemy.

The truth is most believers in the West don't think much about the dynamics of the spiritual battle we live in. There are three types of attack I want us to understand. The first attack is an indirect attack.

These attacks come through sickness, confusion, and division. Paul calls the enemy "the prince of the power of the air" (Eph. 2:2) because the enemy has a certain authority to wage battle for the time being. It won't always be like this, but only for a season.

It may sound odd to attribute sickness, confusion, and division to the work of the enemy, but this is what Jesus did when He was on the earth. Jesus corrected any attempts to blame God for sickness in individuals. Confusion and division also can be an attack from the enemy. This is important so we don't incorrectly direct enmity at other people. You know who your enemy is: Satan and his demons.

The second type of attack in this spiritual battle is also an indirect attack, but it's an attack on our view of God. The enemy loves to incite questions in our hearts about the trustworthiness of King Jesus. In the garden of Eden, the serpent tempted Eve to question God's character. He said, "Did God actually say, 'You shall not eat of any tree in the garden?'" (Gen. 3:1). Then the serpent takes it further by saying, "For God knows that when you eat of it your eyes will be opened, and you will be like God, knowing good and evil" (Gen. 3:5). The line of thought undergirding this lie is that we are the best leaders for our own life. The enemy attacks us with thoughts that bring into question God's character.

The enemy's strategy is the same today. Individuals surrender their life to Christ, but before too long—as life squeezes—the temptation to take back the reins is planted in our minds. Did God really mean surrender? Maybe God doesn't trust you. Maybe God is keeping something from you. We may look at the world and think other people have a care-free and happy life and wonder why we have problems. And before we know it, we are questioning God's character and perfect leadership in our lives.

The third type of attack is on our view of our identity in Christ. Buried below attacks on God's character, and direct attacks the enemy throws at us, are the attacks on our view of who we are in God. If the enemy can't deter us with physical or relational attacks or lies about the character of God, then he will try to deter us by holding us back in a place of fear, insecurity, and doubt. Paul tells us, "Be imitators of God, as beloved children. And walk in love, as Christ loved us and gave himself up for us" (Eph. 5:1-2). John says, "Beloved, do not believe every spirit, but test the spirits to see whether they are from God...Little children, you are from God and have overcome them, for He who is in you is greater than He who is in the world" (1 John 4:1, 4).

We don't live as we ought when we stop living as children of the King. The best place we can be is abiding in the love and mercy of the King. The enemy would love for us to stay held captive in an immature understanding of our position in the King.

THE BATTLE WITH THE FLESH

Another aspect of this battle is within us—a battle with the flesh. This is the famous and explicit battle Paul describes in Romans 7. He talks about this struggle "to do what is good, but evil is present within me." He confesses, that "I do not do the good that I want to do but I practice the evil that I do not want to do (Rom. 7:19)".

I remember asking my college pastor about these very dynamics. Why does my flesh still seem so strong? Why doesn't temptation go away? I remember him drawing a picture to illustrate how

God designed us. He explained how God created us in three parts. We are made of body, soul, and spirit. It's easy enough to understand the body. But most people don't readily understand the difference between the soul and spirit. Most theologians describe the soul as including the mind, will, and emotions. This is our intellect, our volition, and our expressive self. Our spirit is our eternal being that gives us the capacity for relationship with God, which sets us apart from the rest of creation. Animals have bodies, and they have a mind, will, and emotions. But they do not have a spirit.

Before we come to know Jesus, our spirit is dormant. We live, move, and exist, only aware of our body and our soul. This is how we learn to survive on this planet. But our spirit is dormant or dead. It's not until we place our faith in King Jesus that our spirit comes alive. Holy Spirit comes to live in us through faith in Jesus, and this part of our being is made alive. This is what it means to be born again.

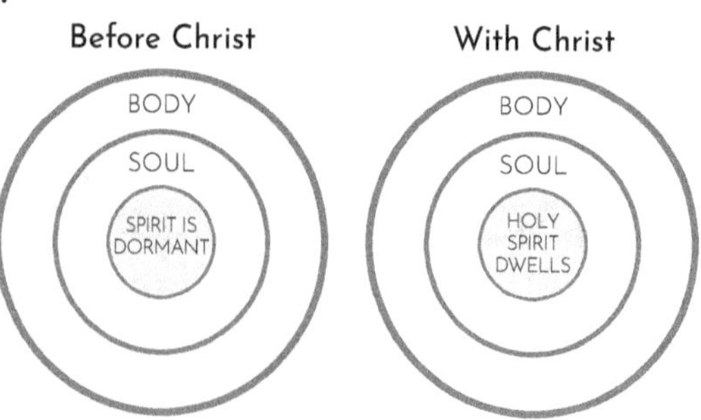

This is why when we first come into the Kingdom, we don't automatically start living perfectly obedient to the ways of King Jesus. The body and the soul that used to call the shots still exist. The difference is that now our spirit is alive. Our spiritual senses are made alive to who God is and His ways for us.

Paul, in talking about the battle with the flesh, goes on to give us hope. He says, "Who will rescue me from this body of death? Thanks be to God through Jesus Christ our Lord!" (Rom. 7:24) He goes onto say, "Therefore there is now no condemnation for those in Christ Jesus, because the law of the Spirit of life in Christ Jesus has set you free from the law of sin and death" (Rom. 8:1-2). We have access to a new way of life. He continues, "For all who are led by the Spirit of God are sons. For you did not receive the spirit of slavery to fall back into fear" (Rom. 8:14-15).

I'm reminded of how John Newton, the pastor, abolitionist, and writer of "Amazing Grace" described this battle. He said,

> You say you feel overwhelmed with guilt
> and a sense of unworthiness? Well, in-

deed you cannot be too aware of the evils inside of yourself, but you may be, indeed you are, improperly controlled and affected by them. You say it is hard to understand how a holy God could accept such an awful person as yourself. You then express not only a low opinion of yourself, which is right, but also too low opinion of the person, work, and promises of the Redeemer, which is wrong. You complain about sin, but when I look at your complaints, they are so full of self-righteousness, unbelief, pride, and impatience that they are little better than the worst evils you complain of. [14]

We are no longer bound to the flesh as we used to be. Now we are led by King Jesus through His Spirit living in us. We are victorious because we are following a King that was victorious through the cross and resurrection. Before we knew Jesus, victory was not possible. Now we can choose to be led by the victorious Spirit that lives in us every time attacks or temptations come.

A LIFESTYLE CHANGE

Good King Jesus has come near and invited us into a life of new values and priorities. He rescued us out of slavery and no longer calls us servant, but now calls us friend and co-heir with Christ. He lifted us from the ash heap and positioned us with princes. He's called us into a battle in which He empowers and entrusts us to be vigilant and aware.

There is nothing about this new way of life in the Kingdom that sounds boring. There is nothing about King Jesus's life that could be characterized as apathetic or lazy. That is why the answer for the boredom in the modern church is not gimmicks and games or accumulating things. The answer lies in a discovery of the gospel of Kingdom.

The story of the Son positions us to live victorious over sin, freed from the bondage of slavery and empowered to choose the way of the Son. He's unveiled His rescue story to us and calls us to live commissioned by the King.

I'm reminded of the short book called *The Chocolate Soldier*[15] written by missionary C.T. Studd more than one hundred years ago. It's a challenge to live lives for the Kingdom, devoted and surrendered to the King. He wrote,

Every true Christian is a soldier–of Christ–a hero "par excellence!" Braver than the bravest–scorning the soft seductions of peace and her oft-repeated warnings against hardship, disease, danger, and death, whom he counts among his bosom friends.

The otherwise Christian is a chocolate Christian! Dissolving in water and melting at the smell of fire. "Sweeties" they are! Bonbons, lollipops! Living their lives on a glass dish or in a cardboard box, each clad in his soft clothing, a little frilled white paper to preserve his dear little delicate constitution.

Here are some Portraits of Chocolate Soldiers taken by the Lord Jesus Christ Himself.

"He said, 'I go sir,' and went not." He said he would go to the heathen, but he stuck fast to Christendom instead.

To the Chocolate Christian the very
thought of war brings a violent attack
of ague, while the call to battle always
finds him with the palsy. "I really cannot
move," he says. "I only wish I could,
but I can sing, and here are some of my
favorite lines:

"I must be carried to the skies
    On a flowery bed of ease,
Let others fight to win the prize,
    Or sail thro' bloody seas.

Mark time, Christian heroes,
    Never go to war;
Stop and mind the babies
    Playing on the floor.

Wash and dress and feed them
    Forty times a week.
Till they're roly poly—
    Puddings so to speak.

Round and round the nursery
Let us ambulate,
Sugar and spice and all that's nice
Must be on our slate."

GOD NEVER WAS A CHOCOLATE
MANUFACTURER, AND NEVER
WILL BE. God's men are always heroes.
In Scripture you can trace their giant
foot-tracks down the sands of time.

There is a valiant call to encounter the Son and His
Kingdom and be called into action. There is no
need to sit on the sidelines as a spectator. There is
no need for excuses. Jesus is calling everyone. Step
into the Kingdom and leave the life of slavery and
bondage behind.

Responding to the Love of the Son

Paul uses the image of slavery to describe our lives before we met King Jesus. We were slaves to sin or in bondage. What bondage did He free you from? Write it out and then thank King Jesus for His freedom.

We have always had a propensity to grow apathetic in our relationships with Jesus. We stop experiencing new things and focus only on past battles won. So, what causes you to get distracted or bored in your relationship with Jesus? Are there things vying for your attention?

Take time right now to acknowledge the Son as King over your life. Declare Him to be the perfect leader for your life.

Ask Jesus if there are any parts of your life He doesn't have rule over. Write them down and then surrender those areas of your life to Him.

Are there places in your life you've experienced freedom through surrender in the past? Write them down and then surrender those areas of your life to Him again.

In response to King Jesus, ask Him to show you what your life would look like if you lived completely surrendered to King Jesus and the ways of His Kingdom. Write them down and pray them into your heart.

Hebrew 12:28-29
Therefore let us be grateful for receiving a
kingdom that cannot be shaken, and thus
let us offer to God acceptable worship, with
reverence and awe, for our God is a consuming fire.

Psalm 113:7-8
He raises the poor from the dust and lifts
the needy from the ash heap, to make them
sit with princes, with the princes of his
people.

Romans 6:17-19
Thank God! Once you were slaves of sin,
but now you wholeheartedly obey this
teaching we have given you. Now you are
free from your slavery to sin, and you have
become slaves to righteous living. Because
of the weakness of your human nature, I am
using the illustration of slavery to help you
understand all this. Previously, you let

yourselves be slaves to impurity and lawlessness, which led ever deeper into sin.
Now you must give yourselves to be slaves
to righteous living so that you will become
holy.

Romans 8:18
Now you are free from your slavery to sin,
and you have become slave to righteous
living.

Ephesians 2:4-7
But God, being rich in mercy, because of
the great love with which he loved us, even
when we were dead in our trespasses, made
us alive together with Christ—by grace you
have been saved— and raised us up with
him and seated us with him in the heavenly
places in Christ Jesus, so that in the coming ages he might show the immeasurable
riches of his grace in kindness toward us in
Christ Jesus.

Revelation 7:15-17
Therefore they are before the throne of

God, and serve Him day and night in His temple; and He who sits on the throne will shelter them with His presence. They shall hunger no more, neither thirst anymore; the sun shall not strike them, nor any scorching heat. For the Lamb in the midst of the throne will be their shepherd, and He will guide them to springs of living water, and God will wipe away every tear from their eyes.

Isaiah 57:15
For thus says the One who is high and lifted up, who inhabits eternity, whose name is Holy; "I dwell in the high and holy place, and also with him who is of a contrite and lowly spirit, to revive the spirit of lowly, and to revive the heart of the contrite."

Galatians 5:1
For freedom Christ has set us free; stand firm therefore, and do not submit again to a yoke of slavery.

Love of the Holy Spirit

CHAPTER SEVEN

Encountering the Holy Spirit

Decades ago, A.W. Tozer said, "The doctrine of the Spirit is buried dynamite." He explains, "Our neglect of the doctrine of the blessed Third Person has had and is having serious consequences. For doctrine is dynamite. It must have emphasis sufficiently sharp to detonate it before its power is released." [16]

All too often in the Church, we neglect the practical implications of living in and with the Holy

Spirit. This truth of the New Covenant invades every aspect of our life. I envision the Church being awakened to this reality of life with the Holy Spirit. The power that ensues will be the distinguishing factor that is meant to follow the New Testament Church.

Just as our gospel identity is extravagantly demonstrated through our relationship with the Father and Son, so it is with the Third Person of the Godhead. The life of the Holy Spirit radically introduces a gospel identity that every believer must grasp and experience. Understanding this perspective of our identity unlocks a lifetime of intimacy with God and has a powerful impact on the world around us.

The Psalm 113 story of God raising us up from the ash heap and placing us with princes only gets better and better. God's plan of redemption takes us from irredeemable to redeemed and indwelt by the Holy God Himself. This is the grand adventure and mystery of the New Covenant promise of life with the Holy Spirit. This part of the story has gone unacknowledged for far too long and needs to be encountered by so many across our cities and nation.

NO SMALL THING

One morning (2 Samuel 6) a man named Uzzah heard that King David was moving the ark of the covenant to Jerusalem. It seemed as though the processional may pass by his family's home that day. Uzzah and his father, Abinadab, had recently heard stories about King David and his victory over the Philistines. It seemed that Israel was being ushered into a season of prosperity and peace. Anticipation and excitement brewed. Uzzah and his family began preparing for King David and his company of thousands to pass by.

Then they began to hear a swelling sound of crowds singing, cheering, and playing instruments. That must be King David and the hosts of people with him, bringing the ark of the covenant to Jerusalem. As the crowd got closer, the volume continued to grow—cymbals, trumpets, and tambourines—this was a sound like they had never heard. They saw the ark approaching, being carried on a cart. King David was in front of the ark and seemed to be intent on one thing, worshiping God.

Uzzah ran out and joined the crowd. He began cheering and celebrating God's provision and strength. What an honor that they would pass by his home that day. Right then, one of the oxen pulling the cart stumbled. The cart jerked about, and Uzzah saw the ark begin to lean. Uzzah was sure that the ark would tumble right off the cart and hit the ground. For Uzzah this was unfathomable. This ark was the most holy item on the planet. It was the focal point of Israel's worship and a representation of God's distinct blessing on the nation of Israel.

So Uzzah reached out to steady the ark of the covenant. He caught it, and it remained safely on the cart. But just as quickly as Uzzah had reached out to steady the ark, he fell dead. His life was over. He encountered the reality of the holiness of God. The crowd stopped. King David quickly came to Uzzah's body and inquired about what had happened.

God's perfection has never been compromised. He is the same yesterday today and forever. Uzzah encountered the reality that God is perfectly holy. The wages of sin is death. This became evident to Uzzah that day. But that's not the end of God's story (or God's holiness). God chose to bridge the chasm that was created by sin. His love is so holy that He doesn't compromise His own standards. Instead, He takes it upon Himself to make a way for us to be truly holy.

The Old Testament was a two-way agreement between God and Israel. In this agreement, God set forth requirements for the children of Israel to live by and fulfill in order to come into His presence. At the time, God's presence dwelt in the tabernacle or the temple. The temple was broken down into three parts: the outer court, the inner court, and the Holy of Holies. The Holy of Holies was a dangerous place. People were almost never allowed into the Holy of Holies. Once a year the High Priest could enter into the Holy of Holies on the Day of Atonement, Yom Kippur, and make the atoning sacrifice. Disobedience in the details could cost someone their life in the presence of God.

Jesus came in perfection and fulfilled each and every requirement of the covenant given to Israel. Every prerequisite for entering the presence of God was satisfied by Jesus. Therefore, not only does He save us from receiving the justified consequences of our sinfulness, but He makes it possible for God's presence to come and live inside of us.

KNOWING THE HOLY SPIRIT

This good news from God's Kingdom isn't emphasized enough in the church. God's intention was not just to punch our ticket to heaven. He came to save us for a greater purpose. He came to save us so we would know Him and in fact, host His very Being. He saved us to be a dwelling place for God. In light of the Old Covenant, the radical grace of God revealed through the indwelling presence of the Holy Spirit can seem scandalous.

With that background set, it's important to explore who the Holy Spirit is. Holy Spirit is a person of God that can be known and appreciated. He is not the third most important Person of the Trinity. He is equal to, and in perfect unity with, the Father and the Son. Attributes of Holy Spirit express the mysterious complexities of who God is and what He is like.

Aspects of God revealed in the Holy Spirit are paramount to our understanding of God. It's necessary to understand these aspects of Holy Spirit's personality if we want to grow in intimate relationship with God. These are not parts of God, as though He is a created entity dependent on interworking parts. These "attributes" are ways in which God has revealed Himself. He is the essence of these aspects of life that we know and experience.

God is actively at work. The first mention of the Holy Spirit is in the second verse of the Bible. In the creation account in Genesis 1:2 it says, "The earth was without form and void, and darkness was over the face of the deep. And the Spirit of God was hovering over the face of the waters." The Holy Spirit was the active agent or expression of God doing the creating and configuring to bring about this divine act of forming everything we know and see.

God is power. Throughout Old and New Testament accounts, the Holy Spirit is revealed as an expression of God demonstrating His supernatural and ultimate power. He is the creator of natural laws but also has the sovereign ability to act supernaturally. In the Old Testament, the Holy Spirit comes onto the scene in times of great victory and breakthroughs. That continues in the New Testament as the Holy Spirit is the main character in the powerful New Testament church.

God is comforter. God's nearness to the people of

Israel was a constant grounding truth of distinction that saw them through the most trying times. From the exodus out of Egypt, to wandering in the wilderness, or capturing the Promised Land, God's constant presence among them was a source of empowering comfort. And as Jesus prepares His followers for the age to come, He describes Holy Spirit as Comforter and Counselor. The Greek word Jesus uses to describe the Holy Spirit in our lives is "parakletos." This is a difficult word for scholars to translate with one word. The word "parakletos" most literally means "called beside or alongside to help." [17] It's the description of an advocate, and that's the reason many translators use the word "counselor".

God is teacher. Jesus tells us that Holy Spirit will come and lead us into all truth, reminding us of all that He taught us. God wants to bring His children along through continual revelation. This single attribute is the defining factor for transformation when it comes to believers actively living the Word of God. Holy Spirit brings God's Word to bear on our personal lives. He opens the eyes of our heart to see properly. He is our teacher.

God is truth. As Jesus is describing the Holy Spirit to come, He says, "The Spirit of Truth, whom the world cannot receive, because it neither sees him nor knows him. You know him, for he dwells with you and will be in you" (John 14:17). Jesus describes the Holy Spirit this way elsewhere as well. The Holy Spirit is the Spirit of Truth. He is the personal agent of truth-bearing and truth-defining. In an age of relativism and personal truth, believers need to know the Spirit of Truth.

God is present. He is everywhere at the same time. Holy Spirit is the living and intimate reminder of God's presence in our lives. We will talk more about this truth in the chapter to come, because the reality of God's always-abiding presence is one of God's primary ambitions in the redemptive plan.

OUR NEGLECT

The 19th century minister Samuel Chadwick wrote, "The root-trouble of the present distress is that the Church has more faith in the world and the flesh than in the Holy Ghost, and things will get no better till we get back to His realized presence and power." [18] This is just as true today.

This one reality of the gospel is both the beginning and the end of our existence of life in God. Life with the Spirit begins through our born-again experience, when Holy Spirit comes and takes up residence in us, resurrecting our spirit that is dead or dormant. The Holy Spirit alive in us is also described as a deposit or seal of the eternal destiny we have in Christ. That means our life with the Holy Spirit keeps us grounded in the eternal life we have with God. It's a foretaste of what is to come.

This fellowship was broken in the Garden of Eden. The Genesis story tells of a garden paradise where Adam and Eve have fellowship and work together with God. That was broken by rebellion and pride. And the Revelation story tells us this fellowship will be restored in the age to come. Revelation 21:3-4 says, "And I heard a loud voice from the throne saying, 'Behold, the dwelling place of God is with man. He will dwell with them, and they will be his people, and God himself will be with them as their God. He will wipe away every tear from their eyes, and death shall be no more, neither shall there be mourning, nor crying, nor pain anymore, for the former things have passed away.'"

The Old Testament backdrop for the New Testament revelation of God's grace tells us that the

Holy Spirit's dwelling within us is something to be cherished. It cannot be a fleeting idea or just a doctrine of words. Our ash heap could not be overcome in any other manner than by the atoning sacrifice of the spotless Lamb. "By sending his own Son in the likeness of sinful flesh and for sin, he condemned sin in the flesh, in order that the righteous requirement of the law might be fulfilled in us, who walk not according to the flesh but according to the Spirit" (Rom. 8:3–4).

Jesus's victory overcoming sin for the sake of forgiveness is one thing, and then that redeemed life becoming the home for God's Spirit is another. These are multiple dimensions of grace let loose in one fell-swoop by the death and resurrection of Jesus. When the veil was torn in the temple on the day of Jesus's crucifixion, it marked the beginning of this New Covenant Age of the Spirit of God no longer living with us or near us in a temple built by human hands, but instead, the Spirit of God coming to take up residence in us. This truth is not just a matter of eternal destination but also a matter for daily life and eternal purpose. This is what we are created for.

CHAPTER EIGHT

A Place for God to Dwell

Growing up, my family's version of vacation was camping. We didn't travel to exotic destinations or stay at fancy hotels; instead, we relaxed by experiencing the great outdoors. We chose to get away by grabbing some tents, a few changes of clothes, and heading to a nearby state park.

I have to admit, now being an adult and having four kids of my own, I do find the idea of camping amusing. People pay money to sleep on the ground in a tiny tent. They willingly submit themselves to the discomforts of muggy weather and mosquitoes in the name of vacation. Don't get me wrong, I love real camping. And by real camping, I mean getting off the grid and going into the wilderness for a pre-determined amount of time. But whether your version of camping is in a luxury RV or backpacking in the wilderness and sleeping in a hammock, the basic fact is that camping is only fun because it's temporary. Camping is not permanent. Camping is about the journey, but it's not the permanent destination.

As we read God's redemptive story in Scripture, we need to keep in mind that God is bringing us somewhere. There is a destination. And it's not so much about the physical destination as much as the end purpose. His intention for humanity is to be with us. In John 17:3, Jesus says, "And this is eternal life, that they may know you, the only true God, and Jesus Christ, whom you sent." And Paul says it like this in 2 Corinthians 6:16, "For we are the temple of the living God; as God said, 'I will make my dwelling among them and walk among them.'"

OUR DESTINY

It's important as we read His redemptive story that we don't lose sight of the end destination. Where is He bringing all of us? It's easy to get off track and focus on unimportant details and miss the most important stuff of Scripture. God has revealed His highest purposes for our existence. It's been revealed throughout history and in the future to come that He is pointing us towards something greater. Our highest purpose is to dwell with God.

This purpose helps make sense of the story of Israel. From the time of Abraham, God has been establishing a people for Himself, that He might dwell with them, and be their sole affection. The ceremonies, requirements, and intentions of the Old Covenant point us to both the New Covenant and to our eternal destiny in the New Heaven and New Earth.

In Exodus 25, God calls Moses to set apart a sacred space or a sanctuary as a place to meet with Israel. God says, "And let them make me a sanctuary, that I may dwell in their midst. Exactly as I show you concerning the pattern of the tabernacle" (Ex. 25:8-9). He goes on to say, "There I will meet with you, and from above the mercy seat, from between two cherubim that are on the ark of the testimony, I will speak with you about all that I will give you in commandment for the people of Israel" (Ex.

25:22).

God is not arbitrary or random. He has an intention and design for everything. He is pointing Israel (and us) toward something—our final destiny with God. He is instructing Moses on how to incrementally point people toward their created destiny. He invoked imagery of heavenly reality in cherubim and precious metals and stones. He is pointing us towards the beautiful work that Jesus has created in the New Covenant.

PRIESTS WITH GOD?

My dad grew up in a devout Catholic family. He went to an all-boys' Catholic high school where he started considering the idea of going into the priesthood. He was interested in God and helping people enough to consider that path of devotion to the Catholic Church. I remember learning that about my dad later in life and the implications hitting me. Boy, I am thankful that my dad did not choose a lifetime of celibacy for the priesthood, but instead pursued a relationship with the woman he would marry. That one decision is the difference between me being here or not.

All joking aside, as we consider the New Covenant that Jesus initiated through His death and resurrection, we see that God has brought us all into the priesthood. And His intentions in our priesthood status are clear—to create worshipers who come directly into the very presence of God. We no longer have to live on the outside looking in. We no longer come through some mediator. We no longer have to sit in the outer courts. We are now ushered into the most Holy Place as priests unto God.

In the Old Testament, God set apart priests as the privileged class of Israelites who got to come into the Holy Place of God. God set up this place on Earth for His glory to dwell. God said, "I will consecrate the tent of meeting and the altar. Aaron also and his sons I will consecrate to serve me as priests. I will dwell among the people of Israel and will be their God. And they shall know that I am the Lord their God, who brought them out of the land of Egypt that I might dwell among them. I am the Lord their God" (Ex. 29:44-46).

We are now a company of priests whose primary purpose is to be in God's presence. As Hebrews tells us, "Since we have confidence to enter the holy places by the blood of Jesus, by the new and living way that he opened for us through the curtain, that is through His flesh, and since we have a great priest over the house of God, let us draw near with a true heart in full assurance of faith, with our hearts sprinkled clean from an evil conscience and our bodies washed with pure water" (Heb. 10:19-22). Or Peter tells us, "But you are a chosen race, a royal priesthood, a holy nation, a people for his own possession, that you may proclaim the excellencies of him who called you out of the darkness into his marvelous light" (1 Pet. 2:9).

We are these priests set apart for the presence of God. He wants to be with us and in us. He gave His life for this. In Revelation, John sees this very image playing out in the future to come. He says that those in Heaven will sing this new song saying, "Worthy are you to take the scroll and to open its seals, for you were slain, and by your blood you ransomed people for God from every tribe and language and people and nation. And you have made them a kingdom and priests to our God, and they shall reign on the earth" (Rev. 5:9-10). Jesus gave His life to usher us into fellowship with Holy Spirit as priests.

THE SPIRIT OF GOD IN THE CHILD OF GOD

There is often confusion about the varying descriptions of the work of the Holy Spirit in believers' lives. Do we receive a part of the Holy Spirit at salvation and need to seek more after the fact? Is the moment of being born again the only experience of the Spirit that is necessary? Are the accounts of baptism in the Holy Spirit in the book of Acts relevant to believers today? I will take time right now to clear up these questions.

When a person discovers the grace of God in Jesus and then surrenders their life to Him, Holy Spirit comes to live inside. This is the "born again" experience that Jesus talks about in John 3. Jesus says, "Unless someone is born again, he cannot see the kingdom of God" (John 3:3). And He goes on to say, "Unless someone is born of water and the Spirit, he cannot enter the Kingdom of God. Whatever is born of the flesh is flesh, and whatever is born of the Spirit is spirit" (John 3:5-6).

Jesus makes clear that our life in God is initiated by a person being "born of the Spirit." The Holy Spirit marks the reality of this adoption into the family of God. At salvation, we are born again by the Holy

Spirit and, specifically, born into a spiritual family. Romans 8:9 says, "You, however, are not in the flesh but in the Spirit, if in fact the Spirit of God *dwells in you.* Anyone who does not have the Spirit does not belong to him" (my emphasis). He makes clear two things: 1) believers need to know that the Spirit of God dwells in us, and 2) we either have the Spirit living in us or we don't. There is no partial Spirit-dwelling.

Galatians 3 and 4 say it beautifully, "But now that faith has come, we are no longer under a guardian, for in Christ Jesus you are all sons of God through faith...And because you are sons, God has sent the Spirit of His Son into our hearts, crying, 'Abba, Father!'" (Gal. 3:25-26; 4:6). Our lives are made holy in the sight of God, and Holy Spirit comes to live in us, confirming the work of grace in our lives and initiating this life of more.

IS THERE MORE?

But is there more? Do we receive everything at salvation? Holy Spirit lives in you at salvation, and everything is made available to us at salvation, but anyone who has been a believer for any amount of time knows that we don't live in the fullness of Holy

Spirit's indwelling presence all the time. Transactionally, we have access to everything at salvation, but—experientially or relationally—we haven't *received* everything at salvation. Let me give a quick example.

In Dennis Bennet's book, *The Holy Spirit and You*, he illustrates this dynamic of *receiving the Holy Spirit* through the following story. Imagine you are expecting a guest in your home to share a meal together and an evening of great conversations. The clock is ticking, and the final preparations are taking longer than expected. You still have some food on the stovetop and the house is still a bit messy. To top it all off, you haven't looked in the mirror lately to make sure you are presentable.

And then you hear the doorbell ring. Your guest is early. You are not ready for him yet. You cry out for your daughter to go and answer the door. You tell her, "Can you go and answer the door? Invite them in and give them the newspaper. Tell him I will be with him shortly." At that point, your guest is in your home, but you have not received him. He is comfortably at home as a welcomed guest, but you haven't actively acknowledged his presence by *receiving* him yet, or by truly hosting him.

Finally, you finish the meal preparations and clean yourself up, and go to the living room to greet your guest and welcome him into your home. You then realize after *receiving* him that he brought you some gifts. It's through a personal welcome that you are able to receive both greater relationship and his gifts. Dennis Bennet says, "The Person of the Holy Spirit has been living in your 'house' ever since your new birth, but now you acknowledge His Presence and receive His gifts." [19]

The book of Acts gives us a narrative of early believers expecting an outpouring of the Holy Spirit resulting in powerful change and gifts, including an intimate prayer language. Some think that the five accounts of the baptism of the Holy Spirit in Acts (Acts 2:1-4, Acts 4:23-31, Acts 9:17-19, Acts 10:44-48, and Acts 19:1-7) are given to mark the beginning of this New Covenant Age, and that believers today shouldn't expect experiences like that. This is such a misreading of Acts!

The book of Acts gives a number of clear understandings of the Holy Spirit's ongoing work in our life.

1) The book of Acts only gives accounts of individ-

uals who already placed their faith in Jesus when receiving the baptism of the Holy Spirit. There is never an instance that equates salvation and baptism of the Holy Spirit.

2) The book of Acts gives accounts of the baptism of the Holy Spirit being poured out on Jews, Samaritans (partial Jews), and Gentiles (non-Jews), demonstrating that God is pouring out His Holy Spirit on *all* people.

3) The book of Acts gives three explicit and two implicit accounts of the baptism of the Holy Spirit being accompanied by an ability to pray in tongues or a language that is not their own.

4) The book of Acts gives us an understanding of the church's ongoing need for the filling of the Holy Spirit for the sake of the mission. We see this through the fresh filling of the Holy Spirit in Acts 4 among believers who already experienced the baptism of the Holy Spirit. And we see it through the necessity for leadership to be "filled with the Holy Spirit" (Acts 6:3).

I take time to say all of this to unlock a hunger in your heart for all that God has for you. Our new life in Christ marks the beginning of a life of ongoing intimate friendship with the Holy Spirit, where we experience Him empowering us, walking with us, filling us, and renewing us daily. The best is yet to come!

GOD'S DWELLING PLACE

Our gospel identity points us toward our future and invites us into a vibrant life of relationship and obedience with God today. Our life in Christ is immersed in purpose and eternity in a way that impacts every aspect of our day-to-day life.

Everyone feels common. Everyone knows where they came from and that they put their pants on one leg at a time. There doesn't seem to be anything special about me. I grew up in North Dakota. The most common reaction I get from people regarding my home state is, "That's where the faces are cut in the side of the mountain, right?" I smile and kindly correct them, informing them that Mount Rushmore is actually more than five hundred miles away in South Dakota. I am from a place not really known for much. My life is common, right?

But isn't that all of us? Our commonness can easily

lull us into believing that God's good news doesn't mean anything for our life. "Yes, it's good news, but not for my day-to-day life," we might think.

This human tendency was at the heart of many of Israel's struggles in the Old Testament. There is always the temptation to profane that which is sacred, or to devalue the holy. Israel is a nation marked by God. Their distinction was God's presence in their midst. Remember Moses pleading with God regarding their wilderness wandering: Moses said, "If your presence will not go with me, do not bring us up from here. For how shall it be known that I have found favor in your sight, I and your people? Is it not in your going with us, so that we are distinct, I and your people, from every other people on the face of the earth?" (Ex. 33:15-16).

God's presence in their midst led them out of slavery in Egypt—both by His mighty hand, and His presence through the pillar of cloud by day and the pillar of fire by night. God dwelling in their midst was their distinction. Israel's forgetfulness can be dumbfounding for us as twenty-first century readers. His manifest presence resided among them as a fire or as a glorious cloud, or through miraculous provision. But time and time again, their restless hearts devalued the favor of God to the point that they grumbled and complained or took matters into their own hands.

How often do we live as though the indwelling presence of God is common? How often do we devalue the sacred in our life? The Holy God of the universe has chosen to redeem us and actually come and dwell in us. This is God's story of "lifting us from the ashes and placing us with princes."

THE HEIGHTS OF HIS GLORY

God's favor on my life is evident because of the Holy Spirit. The Holy Spirit is proof of a down payment on the high value Christ placed on my life. The distinctive characteristic of God's people is now the distinctive characteristic over my life.

The extravagance of God's love isn't just in the forgiveness of our sins but also in the value placed on that redeemed life to host God's presence. These are the heights of God's love that I pray each and every believer would walk in greater understanding of.

I echo the prayer of the Apostle Paul in Ephesians 3:18-19, where he prays that you, "may have strength to comprehend with all the saints what is the breadth and length and height and depth, and to know the love of Christ that surpasses knowledge, that you may be filled with all the fullness of God."

CHAPTER NINE

Hosting His Presence

"Our true nature and personality will never come to fullness apart from His manifest Presence. Learning to host Him is at the center of our assignment, and it must become our focus so that we can have the success He desires before Jesus returns."
—Bill Johnson [20]

Ihope every reader is more convinced than ever of the extravagance of God's love displayed through the Holy Spirit's indwelling presence in our life. This understanding becomes the seat for living in relationship, purpose, and authority in the Holy

Spirit on a daily basis.

I grew up in a church that did a great job of emphasizing the Holy Spirit's work (i.e., His gifts and manifestations). But there wasn't often talk about the Holy Spirit as a person, in whom we have fellowship or relationship. When we only think of what the Holy Spirit does and not of who He is, we lower Holy Spirit to the level of an agent working on behalf of God almighty, as if we were demoting the Holy Spirit to the level of angels.

But Holy Spirit is not lesser than the Father or the Son. As we talked about in Chapter 7, Holy Spirit is a person, and life with Him defines our life on this earth. And this becomes the challenge of a follower of Jesus: to be one who hosts the Presence of God.

AWARENESS

It is easy to misunderstand what is meant scripturally by the phrase "the presence of God." God is *present* everywhere at the same time. But we are not always aware of His present reality. In fact, before we come to faith in Jesus, we are oblivious to the reality of God. Therefore, in Christ, we are invited into a new way of life. It's a life of awareness of God's reality as the dominant reality. When we live with this awareness of God's reality, we step into the presence of God.

The presence of God isn't first and foremost about what we feel. It's about what is true. The uncreated God of the universe is the ultimate reality. So, any time I sin, I turn my back on the truth that God is real or, at a minimum, that His ways are best. Any time I allow worry or anxiety to overcome me, I allow my perception of what is around me to dominate my reality instead of the rule of Jesus.

This does not mean God ever leaves us or is ever not present in our life. It means it is possible (and actually quite common) to step out of God's presence by allowing some other reality to be our dominant reality. For the child of God, sin, fear, anxiety, apathy, depression, victimhood, and addiction are all the result of moments we are focusing on our circumstances, flesh, or preferences. Our life as a child of God isn't about trying harder to impress God; it's about desiring to live with a greater awareness of God's dominant reality in our life.

A Franciscan priest lived four hundred years ago, who was known as Brother Lawrence. His writings were later published in a book titled *The Practice of the Presence of God*, which has become a Christian classic. Describing this life of awareness of God's presence, he says,

> Imagine what contentment and satisfaction he enjoys, possessing such an ever-present treasure! He isn't anxious to find it and doesn't worry about where to look for it, because he has already found it and may take whatever he wants from it. He often calls men blind, complaining that we are content with too little. God has infinite treasures to give us, he says. Why should we be satisfied with a brief moment of worship? With such meager devotion, we restrain the flow of God's abundant grace. If God can find a soul filled with lively faith, He pours His grace into it in a torrent which, having found an open channel, gushes out exuberantly. [21]

God's presence is always there. We just need to be aware of it. His presence is sometimes accompanied by feelings or sensations, but His reality cannot be judged on such superficial things. His reality in a moment is truth, and it is our great aim to live in constant awareness of Him.

Our awareness of His presence is central to our Christian life. It grounds us in our first love and keeps us attuned to the story He has been writing of our lives—as princes brought out of the ashes. As Brennan Manning says, "Just as the failure to be attentive dissolves confidence and communion in a human relationship, so inattention to the Holy unravels the fabric of the divine relationship. Thorns and thistles choke the unused path. A verdant heart becomes a devastated vineyard. As we periodically close off God to our consciousness by looking the other way, our hearts are chilled. Christian agnostics don't deny a personal God; they display their unbelief by ignoring the sacred." [22]

THIS ONE THING

King David had anything a person would want in this world. He had riches, prestige, and power. He had tasted success and the joy of overcoming insurmountable odds. He had a large family and trusted friends. He had it all. Yet David tells us his greatest desire. He says, "One thing have I asked of the Lord, that will I seek after: that I may dwell in the house of the Lord all the days of my life, to gaze upon the beauty of the Lord and to inquire in his temple" (Ps. 27:4).

He only desired to be with God. And for David, that meant being in the inner courts of the tabernacle. He didn't have the great privilege that we have to host God. Instead, he needed to draw near to God by physically being in the place that hosted God's presence. And as David surveyed the world and his life, he knew the *one thing* he desired most was God's presence. The place of greatest fulfillment and joy was in the presence of God.

I often wonder what would happen in the church if we again discovered this fundamental purpose for our existence. What would fade away? What complexities would be resolved by gazing upon God and God alone? I imagine joy returning to the life of believers as we stop chasing after other things to satisfy us. I imagine the clarity of the gospel piercing through the darkness of our world as the goodness of God becomes more evident upon our lives.

The modern church loves to sound sophisticated. We puff ourselves up with psychology and leadership theories that tickle our egos but result in no fruit. We overcomplicate church life with our systems and efficiency-driven culture and ignore the underlying sense that there must be something more. The one thing the church needs more than anything right now is an awareness and appreciation for the presence of God. God's manifest presence accomplishes more in a human heart and the life of a church in a moment than hundreds of hours of talks, seminars, or musical performances could ever bring about.

We can learn and grow in an ever-evolving world, but we need to make sure we don't abandon our first love. It was the presence of God that first drew us to our Savior. That was the moment when we knew that God was real, that we were in need of an answer for the mess of our life, and that Jesus was the only answer. Only the Holy Spirit can achieve that in a person's life. But then, too often, we quickly forget that first encounter. God's design for our life is to encounter Him as a person through the Holy Spirit and then to live our lives continually in awareness of, and in friendship with, the Holy Spirit. This one thing I desire, that I may dwell in the house of the Lord all the days of my life.

I believe God is calling the church back to revive a simple lifestyle of prayer; it's a newly prioritized value for the presence of God more than anything else. I am writing this book in the midst of a global pandemic that has revealed a lot about what we value and what we trust in. It has been a purifying time for the church. During lockdowns and all the other precautions that come with a pandemic, the church hasn't been allowed to rely on the traditions we have grown accustomed to. Church—as an entertainment product to be consumed—doesn't work when gathering imposes risks. Church—as an event to be attended once a week—isn't relevant when people are filled with fear and anxiety seven days a week. And church—as a spectator's event—doesn't make sense when a world is looking for practical answers.

In light of all of this, some thought-leaders have been saying it's time for the church to pivot. They go on to talk about innovation in media and technology and the need for the church to come alongside the narratives of this world. But the truth is, the church needs to pivot toward the ways of the New Testament church. That means valuing the presence of God, a new reliance on prayer—both individually and corporately—and for the church to live on a daily mission to express God's essence in every sphere of this world.

A RENEWED MIND

Paul tells us, "Be transformed by the renewal of your mind" (Rom. 12:2). We are no longer meant to be conformed to the world around us. Instead, Jesus made it possible for us to be transformed through His gospel work actually renewing our minds, to now be in conformity with what God accomplished for us. His extravagant grace gives us a new beginning.

We were hopelessly lost in our brokenness and sin. The prophet Isaiah says that even our righteousness is like filthy rags before a holy God (Isa. 64:6). But, praise God, because of Jesus's death on the cross and His resurrection, we can be made right with God. And this right standing with God is so radical and thorough that God's Spirit can now come and live in each one of us.

As long as humans have existed, we have looked for holy places. We have gone to holy mediators that bridge the gap between us and a holy God. Jesus broke down this dividing wall to the point that we can now live in relationship with God through His Holy Spirit's indwelling presence in our life. Every day and in every way, God can be our everything. Jesus promised us he will be with us, even to the end of the age (Matt. 28:20). This is a true promise of His indwelling presence in all circumstances.

Imagine I pick up a friend at the airport and greet him on his arrival, grab his bag, and help him get situated in the vehicle for the drive home. But after the initial greeting, I never acknowledge his presence in the vehicle or speak to him. In fact, my actions and body language communicate that I have forgotten he is in the vehicle with me. Sometimes I wonder how often we live like this as believers. We live with an Old Testament paradigm. Sacred spaces and sacred people call us to act a certain way or acknowledge God's reality. But, in the everyday stuff of life, we ignore Him. We live as though the work of the cross does not impact the ordinary.

As I talk with people, I often hear confessions about difficulties they have building a relationship with God. They don't know how to walk in a relationship with God on a daily basis. My common response points them towards getting to know and living in relationship with Holy Spirit. Holy Spirit is commonly thought of as the mystical, oft-neglected person of the Trinity when, in reality, Holy Spirit is the most practical expression of who God is for the twenty-first century believer. Holy Spirit lives with us, and in us, every day. He is our Helper. He is our Peace. He is our Teacher that leads us into all truth. He bears witness about Jesus. Jesus said it was to our advantage that He leave and send the Holy Spirit. It is our great privilege to live in an ongoing relationship with Holy Spirit.

I say often that prayer is a two-way conversation. This can sound scandalous to some, but it's only scandalous if we haven't yet understood the goodness of the gospel to redeem us so fully that Holy Spirit comes to dwell in us. From that moment on, we have the opportunity to live in a state that is awake to God, conscious of Him, and being led by Him. The foundation for God speaking to His children is through Scripture. Please understand, without the Holy Spirit, the Bible is just words on a page. But with the Holy Spirit, Scripture is made alive and cuts to our hearts. We start to remember Scripture throughout our day. We might have read a passage a hundred times, and God allows us to read it as though it's the first time we have laid eyes on it. That is the goodness of living life with Holy

Spirit.

From the foundation of a Scripture-saturated life in-dwelt by the Holy Spirit, we begin to realize that there is not a single moment or aspect of our life that God doesn't care about. He cares about it all. And His truth is meant to be a north star for the believer that allows us to rise above the winds and waves of life, to see clearly through it all. Relationship with the Holy Spirit is abundant life that Jesus paid for.

A.W. Tozer said, "Only the Spirit can save us from the numbing un-reality of Spiritless Christianity. Only the Spirit can show us the Father and the Son. Only the in-working of the Spirit's power can discover to us the solemn majesty and the heart ravishing majesty of the Triune God." [23]

The value-affirming purpose placed upon every life is the capacity to host God's presence. It's only possible through Jesus Christ, but all fulfillment, joy, and peace are found in this purpose. The people of Israel ran from or ignored that purpose many times, and it always ended in devastation. Sometimes they chose to idolize the immediacy of the physical (Ex. 32:1-4). Other times they chose to idolize the life they came from in Egypt and ignore the presence of God in their midst (Num. 14:1-4). And still other times, they chose to literally worship other gods and be drawn away by the purposes of neighboring nations (Deut. 30:17-20). Later in Israel's story, they abandoned the higher purposes of God for the low purpose of mere survival. They left the temple of God in ruins and instead chose to build their own paneled houses (Hag. 1:1-6).

All other pursuits leave us empty. God is our highest purpose, and the privilege of hosting Him becomes the expression of a life well lived. No circumstance can steal this from us. No trial or tribulation can hijack this. Our eternal purpose is also our daily purpose.

We host His presence and therefore are the "fragrance of Christ" (2 Cor. 2:15) in the spheres God brings us. We are different in this world because of His presence in us. Change happens in the world around us because of God in us.

Too often, Christians think that the key to cultural transformation or influence in the world is more mobilizing. Without the proper foundation in Christ, this thinking of "do first, be second" can actually cause more damage than good. The way of Jesus is "be first, and then do." We first become immersed in Holy Spirit's life-giving power, and then—with compassion and love—we learn to live in a world that is headed toward destruction.

Authority just is. It's not always recognized, but it is. God's ways sometimes look small and insignificant in the world's eyes, but they carry authority because they are God's ways. God has chosen to carry heavenly treasures of His presence in clay vessels (2 Cor. 4:7-12) as a way of confounding the thinkers of our day. The strength of God is made evident in human weakness. And greatness is demonstrated through radical servanthood. God wants believers to live in His authority, which will turn the world upside down.

As believers, we don't need permission to be a light in the darkness. Either we carry the fire of God in us, or we don't. We don't need to wait for the world to ask us for our thoughts on the issues of our day; we have the answer in Jesus and the only hope living inside of us. We don't need to panic when the world exudes darkness; that is what darkness does. Instead, we choose to walk more in tune with the Holy Spirit and live in such a way that pushes back the enemy. We no longer view the church as an entity just surviving; we understand the Church as a company of people who host God's presence and carry the promise of the Father to a lost and dying world.

Responding to the Love of the Holy Spirit

Take a moment to meditate on God's holiness. Now Jesus has made us holy because of His finished work. Holy means set apart. How have you been transformed and set apart? Think about how you used to think, act, and talk before you knew Jesus. How has that changed? Write it down and be specific.

Do you struggle to think of Holy Spirit as a person? How do you think that has affected how you interact and treat Him?

Look back at the attributes of Holy Spirit on pages 121-123. Take time to thank God for revealing Himself in that way to you.

Do you believe God has purpose for us? How would you define God's purpose for your life? If you are unsure, ask Him to show you and write it down.

Do you live with a consistent awareness of God in your life? If you do, what are you doing to foster that awareness? If you struggle with living in that place of awareness of God, what do you think is keeping you from it?

How do you want to grow in your awareness of God's presence in your life? Think of practical ways to grow in your awareness of Him. Write it down and make a plan to daily grow in your awareness of God.

John 14:16-17
And I will ask the Father, and he will give
you another Helper, to be with you forever,
even the Spirit of truth, whom the world
cannot receive, because it neither sees
him nor knows him. You know him, for he
dwells with you and will be in you.

Romans 8:3-4
For God has done what the law, weakened
by the flesh, could not do. By sending his
own Son in the likeness of sinful flesh and
for sin, he condemned sin in the flesh, in
order that the righteous requirement of the
law might be fulfilled in us, who walk not
according to the flesh but according to the
Spirit.

2 Corinthians 6:16
What agreement has the temple of God with
idols? For we are the temple of the living
God; as God said, "I will make my dwelling

among them and walk among them, and I
will be their God, and they shall be my
people."

Hebrews 10:19-23
Therefore, brothers, since we have confidence to enter the holy places by the blood
of Jesus, by the new and living way that he
opened for us through the curtain, that is,
through his flesh, and since we have a great
priest over the house of God, let us draw
near with a true heart in full assurance of
faith, with our hearts sprinkled clean from
an evil conscience and our bodies washed
with pure water. Let us hold fast the confession of our hope without wavering, for he
who promised is faithful.

Ephesians 2:18-22
For through him we both have access in one
Spirit to the Father. So then you are no
longer strangers and aliens, but you are fel-
low citizens with the saints and members of
the household of God, built on the founda-

tion of the apostles and prophets, Christ Jesus himself being the cornerstone, in whom the whole structure, being joined together, grows into a holy temple in the Lord. In him you also are being built together into a dwelling place for God by the Spirit.

Conclusion

How do we bring all this together? We've been on a journey—really just the beginning of a journey—unpacking the beauty of the gospel. But then, where do we go from here?

We've learned we are adopted, co-heirs of Christ, who host the very presence of God. C.S. Lewis talks about relating to this God who has revealed Himself as Father, Son, and Holy Spirit in terms of a dance. This is a helpful and inspiring description of the adventure we are living in the gospel. It's not an educational or mental pursuit. It's not a boring catechism. It's not a religious exercise. It's a dance.

Lewis said, "And now, what does it all matter? It matters more than anything else in the world. The whole dance, or drama, or pattern of this three-Personal life is to be played out in each one of us; or (putting it the other way round) each one of us has got to enter that pattern, take his place in that dance. There is no other way to the happiness for which we were made." [24]

We have to jump into this dance or cadence of the gospel. The good news of Jesus calls us into an eternity (which is already in motion) of knowing Him in His fullness. He is God the Father, the Son, and the Holy Spirit, personally and profoundly making Himself known to us since the beginning.

If you don't know how to jump into the dance, then I encourage you to immerse yourself in God. Take inventory of the rhythms, sounds, messages, and inspirations that drive you. The more we feed on the truth of the gospel and what God says about us, the more we will begin to move in rhythm with God. We can't have it both ways. We jump into the dance and allow our souls to begin to come alive to truth, and—before we know it—the trajectory of our entire life has changed.

The gospel points us to God. This book was not meant to be an end in itself, but rather a catalyst for more. Too many times, we cheapen the gospel as a quick-fix or instant answer for the ails of our life. The message of the gospel opens the door to a journey of knowing, walking with, and dancing with God. I'm glad you are on the journey with me!

End Notes

1.   Norman Grubb, *C.T. Studd – Cricketer and Pioneer* (Fort Washington, Pennsylvania: Christian Literature Crusade, 21st Edition, 1965), pg. 36.

2.   Dietrich Bonhoeffer, *The Cost of Discipleship* (New York, New York: Simon & Schuster, 1995 edition) pg. 270.

3.   John Stott, *Why I am a Christian* (Downers Grove, Illinois: InterVarsity Press, 2003), pg. 14.

4.   Wayne Parker, "Statistics on Fatherless Children in America" (www.liveabout.com/fatherless-children-america-statistics-1270392), accessed 19 July 2020.

5.   Brennan Manning, *Abba's Child* (Colorado Springs, Colorado: NavPress, 2002) pg. 74.

6.   A.W. Tozer, *God's Pursuit of Man* (Camp Hill, Pennsylvania: WingSpread Publishers, 2007), pg. 4.

7.   L.K. Crocker, "Ceremonial Holiness", *Lexham Bible Dictionary* (Bellingham, Washington: Lexham Press, 2016).

8.   C.S. Lewis, *Mere Christianity* (San Francisco, California: Harper Collins, 2000), pg. 31.

9.   Jack Frost, *Spiritual Slavery to Spiritual Sonship* (Shippensburg, Pennsylvania: Destiny Image Publishers, 2006), pg. 120.

10.   Francis Schaeffer, *True Spirituality* (Wheaton, Illinois: Tyndale House Publishers, 1983), pg. 76.

11.   John Stott, *The Message of Galatians* (Nottingham, United Kingdom: Inter-Varsity Press, 1968).

12.   C.S. Lewis, *The Horse and His Boy* (New York, New York: Harper Collins, 2004), pg. 182.

13.   Guy Duffield & N.M. Van Cleave, *Foundations of Pentecostal Theology* (Los Angeles, California: L.I.F.E. Bible College, 1983), pg. 443.

14.   John Newton, *The Works of Reverend John Newton* (Edinburgh: Banner of Truth, 1985), pg. 185.

15.   C.T. Studd, *The Chocolate Soldier* (Washington, Pennsylvania: Christian Literature Crusade, 2012 edition), pg. 1.

16.   A.W. Tozer, *God's Pursuit of Man* (Camp Hill, Pennsylvania: WingSpread Publishers, 2007), pg. 61.

17.   Dockery, D. S. "Christ as King", *Holman Illustrated Bible Dictionary*, C. Brand, C. Draper, A. England, S. Bond, E. R. Clendenen, & T. C. Butler (Eds.) (Nashville, TN: Holman Bible Publishers), pg. 32.

18.   Samuel Chadwick, *The Way of Pentecost* (Berne, Indiana: Light and Hope Publications, 1959), pg. 13.

19.   Dennis Bennett, *The Holy Spirit and You* (Plainfield, New Jersey: Logos International, 1971), pg. 20.

20.   Bill Johnson, *Hosting the Presence* (Shippensburg,

Pennsylvania: Destiny Image, 2012), pg. 28.

21.	Brother Lawrence, *The Practice of His Presence* (New Kensington, Pennsylvania: Whitaker House, 1982), pg. 26.

22.	Brennan Manning, *The Ragamuffin Gospel* (Sisters, Oregon: Multnomah Press, 2000), pg. 179.

23.	A.W. Tozer, *God's Pursuit of Man* (Camp Hill, Pennsylvania: WingSpread Publishers, 2007), pg. 94.

24.	C.S. Lewis, *Mere Christianity* (San Francisco, California: Harper Collins, 2000), pg. 176.

Acknowledgements

I want to take a moment to express gratitude to a number of people who made this project possible. My wife Tanya has always been my biggest encourager. She pushes me and knows how to remind me of truth. Tanya, I'm so thankful for you! I want to thank the incredible team of world-changers at LifePointe. It's a dream to be doing this alongside each of you. Tony and Kayla Meyer, Kyle and Nicole Barnes, Alex and Katie Rosinger, Riley and Shena Edwards, thank you for processing and helping make this project better. A huge thanks to those who poured over manuscripts and gave feedback for maximum impact - specifically Erin Thompson, Tony Meyer, and our Elder team; Inya Nlenanya and Connie Sloan. Thanks to each of you! And once again, I want to express gratitude to Laura Saunders. Your editorial skills are invaluable, and your willingness to patiently wade through all the details is so appreciated. Thanks to Abbi Beckett for her attention to detail and proofreading skills (and short timeline). And a huge thank you to Kayla Meyer for her expertise on the layout and final print details. I couldn't have completed this without you.

"Blessed is the man who gets to be a part of something bigger than himself and finds himself surrounded by friends who share his same passion."
- Andy Stanley

www.ingramcontent.com/pod-product-compliance
Lightning Source LLC
Chambersburg PA
CBHW070801160726
48004CB00001B/280